SO YOU THINK YOU'RE A PHILADELPHIA EAGLES FAN?

STARS, STATS, RECORDS, AND MEMORIES FOR TRUE DIEHARDS

SKIP CLAYTON

FOREWORD BY MERRILL REESE

SPORTS PUBLISHING

Sports Publishing books may be purchased in bulk at special discounts for sales promotion, corporate gifts, fund-raising, or educational purposes. Special editions can also be created to specifications. For details, contact the Special Sales Department, Sports Publishing, 307 West 36th Street, 11th Floor, New York, NY 10018 or sportspubbooks@skyhorsepublishing.com.

Sports Publishing® is a registered trademark of Skyhorse Publishing, Inc.®, a Delaware corporation.

Visit our website at www.sportspubbooks.com.

10 9 8 7 6

Library of Congress Cataloging-in-Publication Data is available on file.

Cover design by Tom Lau
Cover photo credit: Associated Press

ISBN: 978-1-68358-095-9
Ebook ISBN: 978-1-68358-096-6

Printed in the United States of America

To my wife, Joanne, who is a tower of strength and is always there for me when needed, especially for all the hours that it took to write this book. She has always been behind me 100 percent for all our time together.

To the memory of my mother, Natalie, and my father, Bill, who I both still miss. My father took me to see my first Eagles game at Shibe Park in 1948. We had season tickets in 1960 and we were there at Franklin Field when the Eagles beat the Packers and won the NFL championship in 1960. My parents were always there for me.

To the memory of my mother-in-law and father-in-law, Rosemary and John Stedeford.

To my stepsons; Mike, his wife Lori, our grandchildren, Kimberly, Anna, and Dominic; to Bill, his wife Linda, our grandson Adam, and our great granddaughters, Lily and Harper Rae; to John and Janet and to Jason, Gretchen, and Tyler.

I love them all.

Contents

Foreword by Merrill Reese   *vii*

Introduction   *ix*

First Quarter: Rookie Level   1

Second Quarter: Starter Level   41

Third Quarter: All-Pro Level   77

Fourth Quarter: Hall of Fame Level   105

Acknowledgments   *161*

About the Author   *163*

Foreword

Skip Clayton is an original. An original what, I'm not sure. But nobody else is quite like him. Skip and I have been friends forever. He's also been a great part of WBCB Radio in Levittown, Pennsylvania ever since I have been an owner of the station. That's about twenty-five years.

When Skip wanders in on Mondays at about noon to get ready for his five o'clock *Racing Wrap*, I know that my peace and quiet are about to end. The Skipper launches into a barrage of trivia that causes your head to spin and your thoughts jog back anywhere in Eagles history.

There's a reason my late friend, former Phillies Hall of Fame broadcaster Harry Kalas dubbed him "Memory Lane." Skip has been a fixture in these parts for a long time and his passion for our teams has been unbelievable. His memory is razor sharp. That's also one of my strengths, so when he starts firing Eagles questions, I am up for the challenge.

When he mentioned he was doing a book on Eagles trivia facts and records, I knew it would be packed with a lot more than just dates and scores. This man does his research.

For those of us who go back a ways, it will rekindle some fond remembrances. For young fans, it will prove enlightening.

When Skip Clayton takes on a project, the result is always a winner.

—Merrill Reese
Play-by-play voice of the Philadelphia Eagles
Philadelphia Eagles Hall of Fame, 2016

Introduction

After all these years it is still surprising that among the four major Philadelphia sports teams, the Eagles have gone the longest without a championship parade, but they remain the most popular team in town. They were never a tough ticket from the time they started play in 1933 up through 1959. It was always possible to get good tickets on game day. But that all changed in 1960 when the Eagles won their third and most recent NFL championship by beating the Green Bay Packers. Home games at Franklin Field started to sell out in 1961. Since that time, the Eagles started to take over the town. There were bad times where they had only one winning season between 1962 and 1977, but the fans were still coming to the games. You didn't dare give up your season tickets. Their television ratings go through the roof regardless of what time of day or night they play. Big crowds even come to watch them practice in training camp. They haven't won the Super Bowl yet and, to make matters worse, three expansion teams currently playing in the National Football Conference that came into the league after 1960 have won the Super Bowl—New Orleans, Seattle, and Tampa Bay.

I remember my dad taking me to my first Eagles game at Shibe Park in 1948. What a great year to start following the Eagles as they went on to win their first NFL championship that season.

One thing that I have forgotten was the first team I saw the Eagles play. I remember the score, 45–0, but the problem was the Eagles won three games that year by that exact score, with two of them being home games. It was either against the Boston Yanks or the Washington Redskins. It felt strange seeing a football game at Shibe Park. The field ran from the first base line to left field, and instead of seeing Del Ennis, Willie Jones, and Andy Seminick hitting home runs into the upper deck for the Phillies, it was Cliff Patton kicking extra points and field goals into the upper deck. Like all young guys, we had our favorite players, and mine were Steve Van Buren, easily one of the greatest running backs in NFL history, and Tommy Thompson, one of the greatest Eagles quarterbacks.

My parents and I joined St. Luke's Episcopal Church in Germantown, and I was in the men and boys choir from 1947 to 1952. I am still a member there with my wife, Joanne. I still can remember Father Steele, who was the rector, had a dinner for the choir one night after Christmas and Frank Reagan, one of great players for Penn who would later join the Eagles to help them win the 1949 NFL championship, was our after dinner speaker. I still remember that night like it was yesterday.

It was great that the Eagles came back and won the 1949 NFL championship and were the only team to post back-to-back shutouts in championship games.

Things went downhill from there and it wasn't until 1960 that the Eagles won their third NFL title. That season was the most exciting and my favorite. The Eagles were picked to finish no better than third or fourth in the Eastern Conference behind Cleveland and the New York Giants who had divided all the conference titles from 1950 to 1959 and went back to doing the same from 1961 to 1965. During the 1950s, Cleveland won three NFL championships and New York one.

This was the third season that the club was playing at Franklin Field. We had season tickets during that time and when the Eagles got to play Green Bay for the 1960 championship, we had first choice of seats for the game.

No one knew at the time that the Packers had a dynasty in the making. In fact, the Packers were favored to win the game but this was the year the Eagles were not going to be denied. Philadelphia won 11 games, counting the win over the Packers. No other team in the NFL won more than eight. They sold out only one regular season game at Franklin Field in 1960 but in 1961, sold out six of seven, and sellouts or close to sellouts became the rule rather than the exception.

We kept our season tickets through 1968, and when I became the Sports Director of WRCP Radio before the 1969 season, I began sitting in the press box where I remained through the 2006 season. I had seen a lot of football games at Franklin Field, and I remember sitting in the stands wondering what it would be like to sit up there. Walking up to the press box was no big deal since I was used to climbing the steps to get to our seats.

I was happy to see the Eagles move to Veterans Stadium in 1971 for a variety of reasons. One was it would be warmer on cold days in the press box which would be enclosed. There was no heat in the Franklin Field press box. There was an elevator to get up to the press box, the locker room was four times bigger, and the parking was fifty times better.

I sat through a lot of bad teams from the stands and the press box from 1962 to '75. Things looked up when Dick Vermeil came in 1976, and in his fifth season, the team made it to the Super Bowl. That was a special year to be covering all the Philadelphia teams. The Phillies won the World Series and the 76ers and Flyers made it to the finals which all went six games.

Things dropped off from 1982 to '85 until Buddy Ryan became coach. In his five years as head coach, the team made it to the playoffs three times (consecutively from 1988 to 1990). When Rich Kotite and Ray Rhodes coached the Eagles between 1991 and '98, they made it to the playoffs three times but won only two games.

Andy Reid's era had to be the best since the days of Greasy Neale. They went back to the NFC Championship Game in his third year and made it to the Super Bowl in his sixth season in 2004 but lost to the New England Patriots, who were the team of the decade.

I was able to cover Phillies, 76ers, and Flyers teams that won championships and had hoped that maybe I would cover an Eagles team that won the Super Bowl.

One thing that has never changed since 1960 is the Eagles have the most loyal fan base anywhere. When the opportunity came to do an Eagles book, I immediately agreed. Looking back at the memories of sitting in the stands and the press box, it has been a great run.

1

FIRST QUARTER
ROOKIE LEVEL

FIRST QUARTER

ROOKIE LEVEL

(Answers begin on page 9)

We begin with simpler questions about the Eagles, from their early years in the 1930s through the eighty-four seasons the team has been in the NFL.

1 Eagles owner Bert Bell came up with the idea of having a draft. He was able to convince other owners in the league at the time including George Halas of the Chicago Bears, Curly Lambeau of the Green Bay Packers, and Tim Mara of the New York Giants to go along with this. What city held the first draft in 1936?

2 Who was the first quarterback that the Eagles drafted who made the Hall of Fame?

3 The NFL once had a special bonus pick in the first round. The team earning the pick had the first overall pick regardless of where they finished. The Eagles won it once. Who did they select?

4 MATCH THESE EAGLES WITH THE YEAR THEY WERE DRAFTED

1.	Bob Brown	a. 1982
2.	Harold Carmichael	b. 1999
3.	Randall Cunningham	c. 1964
4.	Donovan McNabb	d. 1971
5.	Mike Quick	e. 1985

5 MATCH THESE EAGLES WITH THE ROUND THEY WERE DRAFTED

1.	Bobby Walston	a. sixth
2.	Harold Carmichael	b. eighth
3.	John Bunting	c. fourteenth
4.	Wilbert Montgomery	d. seventh
5.	Seth Joyner	e. tenth
6.	Clyde Simmons	f. ninth

6 MATCH THESE EAGLES QUARTERBACKS WITH THE ROUND THEY WERE DRAFTED

1.	Sonny Jurgensen	a. first
2.	Randall Cunningham	b. third
3.	Donovan McNabb	c. fourth
4.	Nick Foles	d. second

7 MATCH THESE EAGLES WITH THEIR CAREER-LEADING CATEGORY

1.	Most Touchdown Passes	a.	Reggie White
2.	Most Rushing Yards	b.	Brian Westbrook
3.	Most Receiving Yards	c.	David Akers
4.	Most Total Yards from Scrimmage	d.	Adrian Burk
5.	Most Sacks	e.	Donovan McNabb
6.	Most Seasons Played	f.	LeSean McCoy
7.	Most Points	g.	Harold Carmichael
8.	Most Punts	h.	Chuck Bednarik

8 When Donovan McNabb became the starting quarterback during the 1999 season, who did he replace?

9 MATCH THESE EAGLES WITH THEIR NICKNAME

1.	Chuck Bednarik	a.	Dutchman
2.	Bob Brown	b.	Smackover
3.	Ron Jaworski	c.	Wildman
4.	Pete Retzlaff	d.	Concrete Charlie
5.	Clyde Scott	e.	Baron
6.	Norm Van Brocklin	f.	The Minister of Defense
7.	Reggie White	g.	The Boomer
8.	Norm Willey	h.	Jaws

10 What player drafted by the Eagles in 1950 didn't join the team until 1951 but played two years in the National Basketball Association with the Minneapolis Lakers instead.

11 Which Maxwell Award winner was drafted by the Eagles in 1956 and was arrested when he came to the banquet to pick up his award?

12 I played on the 1960 Eagles after being drafted by Green Bay in 1959. After playing only one game with the Packers that season, I spent eight years with the Eagles and was traded to the Baltimore Colts in 1968. The last game I played in was Super Bowl III when the Colts were upset by the New York Jets. Later on, I appeared in the both the movie version of *M*A*S*H* and the television series. Who am I?

13 There have been four Eagles head coaches that played for the team. Name them. Hint: All four had also served as assistant coaches with the Eagles.

14 What former Eagles coach won a Super Bowl with another team?

15 Who was the first Eagles coach to win his first three games?

16 Who was the only Eagles coach to be selected to the Pro Football Hall of Fame strictly as a coach?

17 George Allen was credited with the nickel defense, but it originated in Philadelphia. Who was the Eagles assistant coach that devised the five-man backfield?

18 During a home game in 1968, an airplane flew over the field with a sign behind it stating,____Must Go. Who was the coach?

19 Buck Shaw was hired as the Eagles coach in 1958 and was the last Eagles coach to win the NFL championship. Vince McNally interviewed an assistant coach before

hiring Shaw, and he later was voted into the Pro Football Hall of Fame. Who was he?

20 Three former Eagles players later became head coaches and won the Super Bowl. Who were they?

21 Buddy Ryan coached the Eagles from 1986 to '90. Match the player with what Ryan had to say about him.

1. "All he does is catch touchdown passes."	a. Luis Zendejas
2. "He looks like a reject guard out of the USFL."	b. Chris Carter
3. "A medical reject."	c. Earnest Jackson
4. "I would trade him for a six-pack that doesn't have to be cold."	d. Michael Haddix
5. "Why would I try to hurt him?"	e. Keith Byars

22 Of the seven home stadiums that the Eagles have played in, name the only two they won their first game in.

23 During the lifespan of the Eagles, there have been three other professional football teams that have called Philadelphia home. What were they called and what league did they play in?

24 The Eagles have had five players that were voted MVP of the Pro Bowl. Who was the most recent?

25 All the Big 5 schools in college basketball at one time or another had college football teams. Penn, Temple, and Villanova are still fielding teams. La Salle ended its program after 2007 and Saint Joseph's dropped football after the 1939 season. A track star from the Saint Joseph's Hawks made the Eagles roster in 1976. Who was he?

ROOKIE LEVEL ANSWERS

1 Philadelphia was the first city to host the NFL draft at the Ritz-Carlton Hotel in 1936. The draft was held twelve more times there:

1944—Warwick Hotel
1949-1950, 1953-1954, 1956 (first three rounds)—Bellevue-Stratford Hotel
1957—Warwick Hotel (first four rounds)
1958-1961—Warwick Hotel
2017—Benjamin Franklin Parkway

From 1956 to 1959, the NFL had two draft sessions. In the 1957 draft, the Eagles picked right after Cleveland, who took Jim Brown with the sixth pick in the first round. Brown turned out to be arguably the greatest running back in NFL history. The Eagles selected Clarence Peaks followed by Billy Ray Barnes, Tommy McDonald, and Sonny Jurgensen.

2 Sonny Jurgensen from Duke in the fourth round in 1957. They have drafted six quarterbacks in the first round:

1936—Jay Berwanger	University of Chicago
1939—Davey O'Brien	Texas Christian University
1949—Frank Tripuka	University of Notre Dame
1972—John Reaves	University of Florida
1999—Donovan McNabb	Syracuse University
2016—Carson Wentz	North Dakota State University

"That was my best draft in 1957 when we drafted [Clarence] Peaks, [Billy Ray] Barnes, [Tommy] McDonald, and Jurgensen, 1-2-3-4 in that order," said former general manager Vince McNally, "because they all made the club right away. When I talked to Bud Wilkinson, who was the coach at Oklahoma, I said, 'Can you be honest with me about McDonald and what are his chances in pro ball' and he told me he has one chance and put him on the outside where nobody can get near him. Give him a lot of daylight and you are going to have a good football player and that was what we did. I knew that Jurgensen was going to be great because of the information that I got. I sent Charlie Gauer, one of our assistant coaches, down there to Duke to see him." Jurgensen was inducted in the Pro Football Hall of Fame in 1983.

Jay Berwanger never played for the Eagles. The Eagles traded the first recipient of the Heisman Trophy to the Chicago Bears, but Berwanger couldn't come to terms on a contract with them and never played in the NFL.

Davey O'Brien played only the 1939 and 1940 seasons before retiring and joining the FBI. In 1938, O'Brien became the first player to win the Heisman and Maxwell Award in the same year. In his final game against Washington at Griffith Stadium, he set three NFL records at the time for most attempts

Sonny Jurgensen (9) and Tommy McDonald in 1961.
AP Photo/Paul Vathis.

in a game with 60, most completions with 33, and most yards passing with 316. O'Brien also stood out on defense in 1940, intercepting four passes. In 1981, the Davey O'Brien Award was established and is given to the best quarterback in college football.

Frank Tripuka graduated from Notre Dame in 1949 and never played for the Eagles, instead they traded him to the Detroit Lions. His son, Kelly, also a graduate of Notre Dame, made his mark in basketball, playing 10 years in the NBA.

John Reaves spent three years with the Eagles, mostly as a backup to Pete Liske and Roman Gabriel. Reaves was traded to Cincinnati in 1975.

Donovan McNabb spent 11 years with the Eagles and rewrote the Eagles record book for quarterbacks. After the 2009 season, he was traded to Washington, the second time the Eagles sent a top quarterback to Washington (Jurgensen had been traded to the Redskins in 1964).

Carson Wentz was the most recent quarterback to be drafted in the first round, and when Sam Bradford was traded right before the 2016 season began, he took over as the starter and won his first three starts.

3 Chuck Bednarik in 1949.

The National Football League made the first overall pick a bonus pick determined by a lottery starting in 1947. This practice was dropped after 1958. The Eagles would have had the last pick in the first round after winning the championship a year earlier if they hadn't won the lottery for the only time. Bednarik had been a two-time All-American at Penn, won the Maxwell Award as the College Player of the Year, and finished third in voting for the Heisman Trophy in 1948.

Bednarik set the club record for the most years with the Eagles (14). He was selected All-Pro 10 times, was picked for eight Pro Bowls, was selected to the 1950s All-Decade Team as well as the NFL 75th Anniversary All-Time Team. His most memorable moment was being the last of the 60-minute men when he went both ways in the Eagles win over Green Bay at Franklin Field in 1960 to win the NFL championship when he stopped the Packers, Jim Taylor on the eight-yard line on the last play of the game.

4 Here are the answers to Match These Eagles With the Year They Were Drafted:

1. c, Bob Brown (1964)
2. d, Harold Carmichael (1971)
3. a, Mike Quick (1982)
4. e, Randall Cunningham (1985)
5. b, Donovan McNabb (1999)

Brown was taken in the first round with the second overall pick and in his five years with the Eagles made All-Pro in 1965, 1966, and 1968. He was named to the All-Decade team of the 1960s. He was traded to the Los Angeles Rams in 1969. Brown was inducted into the Pro Football Hall of Fame in 2004.

Carmichael spent 13 years with the Eagles and set club records for most passes caught (589), yards receiving (8,978), and touchdowns scored (79). He set the NFL record at the time for the most consecutive games with a pass reception (127). The streak ended in Dallas when he got hurt in the final game of the 1980 season. Harold made the Pro Bowl four times and was the winner of the NFL Man of the Year Award in 1980.

Quick spent nine years with the Eagles and was selected to five Pro Bowls. Quick was not the first receiver they wanted in the draft. They had their sights set on Perry Tuttle, another wide receiver, who was selected by the Buffalo Bills one pick ahead of him. Tuttle did very little in the NFL. He caught 25 passes over three years with three different teams, and Quick had an outstanding career with the Eagles. Injuries cut his career short, and he retired during the 1990 season. Quick ranks third in club history with 6,464 yards receiving and seventh in receptions with 363.

Cunningham was taken by the Eagles in the second round of the 1985 draft and became the starter after ten games of the 1986 season. He made the Pro Bowl three times and was MVP of the 1989 game. Cunningham was the NFC Offensive Player of the Year in 1990, the Comeback Player of the Year in 1992, and won the Bert Bell Award twice with the Eagles.

McNabb's selection in the first round was met with a chorus of boos at Madison Square Garden when the Eagles picked second behind Cleveland, who drafted Tim Couch. Everyone wanted the Eagles to pick running back Ricky Williams, who won the Heisman and the Maxwell Award after setting or tying twenty NCAA records at the University of Texas. Williams went to the New Orleans Saints with the fifth pick, but it was McNabb that had the better career.

Most of the time, when a new coach comes in, he likes to start with his own quarterback. Buck Shaw wanted an experienced quarterback when he took over the Eagles in 1958 so they obtained Norm Van Brocklin from the Los Angeles Rams. Joe Kuharich traded for Norm Snead and sent Sonny Jurgensen packing to Washington. Like Shaw, both Mike McCormack

(Roman Gabriel) and Dick Vermeil (Ron Jaworski) started former Rams quarterbacks. Buddy Ryan preferred Randall Cunningham and Matt Cavanaugh over Jaworski. Ray Rhodes started Rodney Peete ahead of Cunningham. Andy Reid stayed with McNabb for 11 years. McNabb broke just about every Eagles passing record. Reid picked up Michael Vick in 2009 and traded McNabb to Washington after the season. When Chip Kelly took over from Reid in 2013, he stayed with Michael Vick for six games until he replaced him with Nick Foles for the rest of the season. Foles was still the starter when 2014 began, but he suffered a broken collarbone midway through the season. Mark Sanchez replaced him, and before the 2015 season began, Kelly went out and got his own quarterback when he traded for Sam Bradford, who lasted only one season. Doug Pederson came in and, right before the 2016 season began, sent Bradford to the Vikings and went with his own quarterback, Carson Wentz who, like McNabb, was taken with the second pick in the first round of the draft.

5 Here are the answers to Match These Eagles With the Round They Were Drafted:

1. c, Bobby Walston (fourteenth)
2. d, Harold Carmichael (seventh)
3. e, John Bunting (tenth)
4. a, Wilbert Montgomery (sixth)
5. b, Seth Joyner (eighth)
6. f, Clyde Simmons (ninth)

Walston was drafted in the fourteenth round in 1951. He was an outstanding end and made the NFL All-Decade team of the 1950s. He also handled all the placekicking, and he retired with the team record for most points scored with 881. Walston led the league in scoring with 114 points in 1954, and he also set the club record for the most points scored in a game with 25 against Washington that season. Adrian Burk threw seven touchdown passes that day, three to Bobby, who added seven extra points. Twice injuries kept him sidelined as a receiver, but he still was able to kick. He suffered a busted jaw in 1954 and, in his final year in 1962, suffered a broken arm which ended his season as a receiver. Walston never missed a game during his 12-year NFL career, playing in 148. His most famous field goal came in the final 10 seconds in 1960 when the Eagles rallied to beat the Browns in Cleveland, 31–29.

Carmichael was selected in the seventh round in 1971 and played 13 seasons with the Eagles, one short of the club record for the longest tenure. In Carmichael's first two years, he saw limited action as a wide receiver and tight end but beginning in 1973 that all changed. Carmichael played strictly wide receiver and his career took off. That year, he set the club record at the time for the most passes caught in a season with 67. Harold set the club record for the most consecutive games played with 162. After the 1983 season, the Eagles released Carmichael, who signed with the Cowboys. His next step should be a call to Canton, Ohio, and induction into the Pro Football Hall of Fame.

Bunting was selected in the tenth round in 1972. One of the top linebackers in Eagles history, he played in 132 games over 11 seasons, helping them make the playoffs four straight years from 1978 to 1981. Although Bunting was far from the biggest linebacker when he reported to his first training camp, he was an intelligent player and studied film for hours. After Bunting left the Eagles, he spent two years with the Philadelphia Stars and helped them win the 1984 USFL championship. Later on, Bunting was an assistant coach under Dick Vermeil at St. Louis when they won the Super Bowl in the 1999 season.

Montgomery was picked in the sixth round of the 1977 draft. The Eagles made their first selection in the fifth round and had two selections in the sixth round, and he was third player taken by the Eagles. Montgomery spent the season returning kickoffs and in the final game of the year, started his first game at running back and came through rushing for 103 yards against the New York Jets. The Eagles found their best running back since Steve Van Buren retired twenty-five years earlier. After that, Montgomery became the first Philadelphia player to rush for 1,000 yards in consecutive seasons in 1978 and 1979 when he set the club record with 1,512 yards rushing (since broken by LeSean McCoy with 1,607 in 2013). Montgomery rushed for over 1,402 yards in 1981, becoming the first Eagle to rush for 1,000 or more yards in a season three times. His biggest game was the 1980 NFC Championship Game when he ran for 194 yards, two yards short of the team record set by Van Buren in the 1949 NFL Championship Game against the Rams in Los Angeles. On the Eagles' second play of the game, Montgomery scored on a 42-yard run as the Eagles went on to beat the Cowboys at the Vet, 20–7. After the 1984 season, Montgomery was traded to the Lions.

The Eagles had two selections in the eighth round of the 1986 draft, and Joyner was second player taken by the Eagles in that round. He went on to become one of the all-time greatest Eagles linebackers. Joyner was cut during his first training camp but was later re-signed during the season. He went on to make All-Pro three times (1991–93), was selected to the Pro Bowl three times, and was selected as the *Sports Illustrated* NFL Defensive Player of the year in 1991. That year against Houston, Joyner recorded eight solo tackles, two forced fumbles, two fumble recoveries, and two sacks despite having a temperature of 102 as the Eagles defeated the Oilers, 13–6. Joyner stayed with the Eagles through 1993. He played out his option and joined his old coach, Buddy Ryan, with the Cardinals. His final game was as a member of the Denver Broncos when they won the Super Bowl over Green Bay in January 1998. Joyner was selected to the Eagles 75th Anniversary Team.

Simmons was taken in the ninth round of the 1986 draft, one round after Joyner. That was Buddy Ryan's first draft, and he came away with three players who all made the Eagles 75th Anniversary Team (Simmons, Joyner, and Keith Byars). With Reggie White on one side of the defensive line and Simmons on the other, the Eagles defense was imposing. Simmons spent his first eight years with the Eagles before joining Ryan in Arizona. He led the NFL in sacks with 19 in 1992 and finished his career with 121.5 sacks, 20th best in NFL history. He ranks third all-time in club history with 76. Simmons scored three touchdowns with the Eagles, two on fumble returns, but his third was his biggest in 1988 against the Giants at the Meadowlands. Luis Zendejas lined up to attempt a field goal in overtime, but it was blocked. Simmons grabbed the ball and returned it 15 yards for a game-winning touchdown. This enabled the Eagles to go to 7–5 and tie the Giants and the Cardinals for first place.

6 Here are the answers to Match These Eagles Quarterbacks With the Round They Were Drafted:

1. c, Sonny Jurgensen (fourth)
2. d, Randall Cunningham (second)
3. a, Donovan McNabb (first)
4. b, Nick Foles (third)

Jurgensen was selected in the fourth round in 1957. Vince McNally's first four choices that year all played in the backfield. Fullback Clarence Peaks was taken in the first round followed by halfbacks Billy Ray Barnes and Tommy McDonald. The Eagles needed help all over after going 4–7–1 and 3–8–1 in 1955 and 1956. A quarterback was badly needed. Adrian Burk had retired and Bobby Thomason wasn't the answer. No running back had gained over 500 yards in a season for the Eagles since 1950. Jurgensen started four games and was 3–1. His first start came in the fourth game of the season against the Cleveland Browns at Connie Mack Stadium. After Bobby Walston kicked a 12-yard field goal in the first quarter, Jurgensen threw a 46-yard touchdown pass to Rocky Ryan and scored on a 1-yard quarterback sneak in the fourth quarter as the Eagles won, 17–7. After sitting on the bench behind Norm Van Brocklin for three years beginning in 1958, Jurgensen became the starter in 1961 and set a new NFL record for most yards passing with 3,723 and tied the NFL record for most touchdown passes with 32. That still remains the club record which Jurgensen set during a 14-game season. The Eagles made one of their worst trades in 1964 when they sent Jurgensen packing to Washington and a trip to the Hall of Fame in 1983. Over the next 11 years, Jurgensen faced his old team 17 times, winning

12 and losing three with two games ending in a tie. His last game against the Eagles was at the Vet in 1974. The Redskins were trailing, 20–7, midway through the third quarter when Jurgensen replaced Billy Kilmer. Washington answered with 20 straight points and Jurgensen completed the scoring with a 30-yard touchdown pass to Charlie Taylor on third and one. Jurgensen has been considered one of the best pure passers in NFL history and was selected to the league's All-Decade team of the 1960s.

Cunningham was taken in the second round of the 1985 draft. When he arrived in Philadelphia, Ron Jaworski was entering his ninth season with the team and Joe Pisarcik had been the backup for the past five years. Jaworski was thirty-four years old and the Eagles were looking to the future. Randall saw action in six games in his rookie year, starting four and posting a 1–3 record. Buddy Ryan came in the following year. Jaworski remained the starter, but on third down and long, Cunningham replaced him. When Jaworski was injured in the tenth game of the season against the Giants at Veterans Stadium, Jaworski was done for the year, and as it turned out, it was his last game with the Eagles. Cunningham took over as the starter. In 1990, he threw the second longest touchdown pass in club history when he connected with Fred Barnett for 95 yards in Buffalo. He also set the club record for most yards rushing in a season by a quarterback with 942, third highest in NFL history. A season-ending injury in the first quarter of the season opener in 1991 at Green Bay kept him out for the remainder of the season. In 1995, Cunningham lost his starting job to Rodney Peete under a new coach, Ray Rhodes. Cunningham retired after the season, but later came back and played five more seasons with Minnesota, Dallas, and Baltimore.

McNabb was drafted in the first round in 1999. Cleveland had the first overall pick and took Tim Couch, a quarterback who never did much in the NFL. McNabb went on to set club records for most pass attempts (4,746), completions (2,801), yards passing (32,873), and touchdown passes (216). He also rushed for 3,249 yards, the second best total for an Eagles quarterback, trailing only Randall Cunningham. In McNabb's 11 years with the Eagles, they made the playoffs eight times, went to the NFC Championship Game five times, and lost the Super Bowl to New England following the 2004 season. McNabb was traded after the 2009 season to Washington.

Foles was selected in the third round in 2012. Michael Vick came in 2009 and was the backup to McNabb in his last year with the team. Vick became the starter in 2010. Foles made his debut against Dallas in Week Thirteen of his rookie season after Vick suffered a head injury. In his third start of the 2013 season, Foles tied the NFL record for the most touchdown passes in a game with seven which also tied the club record set by Adrian Burk in 1954. Foles finished the season with 27 touchdown passes and only two interceptions. His touchdown/interception ratio was the best in NFL history. After posting a 6–2 record as a starter in 2014, Foles broke his collarbone in the eighth game of the season against Houston, ending his year. He was traded to the Rams in a deal that bought Sam Bradford to Philadelphia for one season.

7 Here are the answers to Match These Eagles With Their Career-Leading Category:

1.	Most Touchdown Passes	e.	Donovan McNabb 216
2.	Most Rushing Yards	f.	LeSean McCoy 6,792
3.	Most Receiving Yards	g.	Harold Carmichael 8,978
4.	Most Total Yards from Scrimmage	b.	Brian Westbrook 9,785
5.	Most Sacks	a.	Reggie White 124
6.	Most Seasons Played	h.	Chuck Bednarik 14
7.	Most Points	c.	David Akers 1,323
8.	Most Punts	d.	Adrian Burk 393

Ron Jaworski had held the Eagles record for the most touchdown passes thrown with 175 until McNabb came along. McCoy had broken Wilbert Montgomery's record for the most yards rushing in his final season in 2014 before being traded to Buffalo. Carmichael's record for most yards receiving has held up since 1981, and Westbrook set the record for most total yards from scrimmage in 2009. Reggie White played with the Eagles only eight years, but no one has come close to breaking his record. Bednarik played his fourteenth and final year in 1962. At the time, only two players had played 13 years; Vic Sears, who retired on his own after the 1953 season, and Bucko Kilroy, who suffered a career-ending injury in the season opener in 1955. Later on, Harold Carmichael and Brian Dawkins each spent 13 seasons with the Birds. Of all of these records, Burk's has held up the longest since 1956. He was with team for six seasons when they only played 12 games each year.

8 Doug Pederson started the first nine games in 1999 before Donovan McNabb took over the job for the next 11 years. Pederson was the quarterback for Miami in the 1993 game at Veterans Stadium when Don Shula set the career record for the most wins by a coach with his 325th. The Dolphins had already lost Dan Marino after the fifth week of the season. Scott Mitchell took over and was injured in the third quarter against the Eagles and Pederson came in and led the Dolphins to a 19–14 win. This was only his fourth game in the NFL but his first with the game on the line. Pederson spent 12 years in the NFL as a player before turning to coaching.

Quarterback had become a problem with the Eagles after Rodney Peete led them to the playoffs in 1995 after taking over for Randall Cunningham. They tried both Detmer brothers, Koy and Ty, Mark Rypien, and Bobby Hoying. When Andy Reid took over, he wanted his own quarterback. He picked up Pederson and drafted McNabb.

9 Here are the answers to Match These Eagles With Their Nickname:

1. d, Chuck "Concrete Charlie" Bednarik
2. g, Bob "The Boomer" Brown
3. h, Ron "Jaws" Jaworski
4. e, Pete "Baron" Retzlaff
5. a, Norm "The Dutchman" Van Brocklin
6. f, Reggie "The Minister of Defense" White
7. c, Norm "Wildman" Willey

At one time, NFL players had to work other jobs in the off-season. Bednarik sold concrete and will always be remembered as one of the greatest Eagles players ever. He was inducted into the Pro Football Hall of Fame in 1967.

Brown was the greatest offensive tackle in Eagles history. The Eagles had the second pick in the 1964 draft and he became a perennial All-Pro. When Joe Kuharich was fired in 1969, Brown demanded a trade and was sent to the Rams. He later was voted into the Pro Football Hall of Fame. Brown retired after the 1973 season, but had to wait for the call to Canton until 2004, which was long overdue.

Jaworski was acquired from the Rams in 1977. Dick Vermeil wanted his own quarterback and Jaws played for the Eagles for 10 years, setting quarterback records at the time for the most passing attempts (3,918), most completions (2,088), most yards passing (26,963), and most touchdown passes (175). Donovan McNabb later surpassed those totals.

Retzlaff had an outstanding career with the Eagles (1956–66) as a split end and tight end. He tied Raymond Berry of the Baltimore Colts for the most passes caught in the 1958 season with 56. When he retired, he was the Eagles' leading receiver at the time with 452 catches and 7,412 yards. He went to the Pro Bowl five times.

Van Brocklin came to the Eagles in a trade with the Rams in 1958 and stayed just three years. He was MVP of the NFL in 1960 when the Eagles won the NFL championship over Green Bay. He made the Pro Bowl each season he played in Philadelphia and was the second quarterback at the time to win a championship in his last game (Otto Graham of Cleveland was the first in 1955). Van Brocklin was inducted into the Pro Football Hall of Fame in 1971.

White joined the Eagles in 1985 and stayed eight years. He played 121 games and set the club record for the most sacks with 124. He made the Pro Bowl and was voted All-Pro seven times each. He was inducted into the Pro Football Hall of Fame in 2006.

Willey spent eight seasons in the NFL, all with with the Eagles and made All-Pro three times. He played when sacks were not counted as an official stat. In a 1952 game at the Polo Grounds against the Giants, one account revealed that he tackled New York quarterback Charlie Conerly 17 times attempting to pass as the Eagles won the game, 14–10.

10 Bud Grant.

After playing for the Minneapolis Lakers in 1950 and 1951 (winning an NBA title in his first season), Grant joined the Eagles as a defensive end. In 1952, the Eagles moved Grant to offensive end. He was second in the league in receptions with 56 and yards gained with 997, a club record at the time. He was also the first Eagles player to go over 100 yards receiving four times in a season, and he set the club record for most yards receiving in a game with 203 which held up until 1961 when Tommy McDonald broke it with 237 yards against the Giants. Grant only stayed two years before turning down a contract offer from the Eagles and jumped to the Canadian Football League where he had a great career as a receiver and coach, winning the Grey Cup four times with Winnipeg. In 1967, Grant became the coach of the Vikings for 18 years and became the first coach to take his team to the Super Bowl four times, all losses. Grant was selected to the Pro Football Hall of Fame in 1994.

11 Tommy McDonald.

When McDonald flew into Philadelphia, he was supposed to pick up his rental car at the airport. When the girl behind the counter saw McDonald, she screamed, "It's him!" The next thing he knew, the police came and arrested him. It seems that there was a kissing bandit roaming around, and the girl thought that McDonald was the guy. The police had McDonald up against the wall and ordered him to, "Spread Eagle." McDonald, who had recently been taken in the draft in the third round by the Eagles, said, "No, that's not Spread Eagle. It is Philadelphia Eagles."

He finally convinced the police that he was Tommy McDonald and to check with the Eagles. They did, and he was released. Later, he saw a sketch of the kissing bandit, and it did look a lot like him.

McDonald played with the Eagles for seven years. He held the club records at the time he was traded to Dallas for most yards receiving in a career with 5,499 and caught the most touchdown passes with 66. When he retired after the 1968 season, he ranked second on the NFL career list with 84 touchdown receptions. McDonald was one of the greatest receivers in Eagles history, but he was also known for cutting off his sleeves to have a better reach. There were times he was hit hard, but McDonald always jumped right back up. Why it took him thirty years to get into the Pro Football Hall of Fame was a mystery. Then again, another icon in Philadelphia went through this—Richie Ashburn had to wait thirty-three years after he retired before he was inducted in the Baseball Hall of Fame in 1995.

The Maxwell Football Club later started the Bert Bell Professional Player of the Year Award in 1959. Norm Van Brocklin won it in 1960. Other Eagles winners were Pete Retzlaff, Ron Jaworski, Randall Cunningham, Michael Vick, and Carson Wentz.

12 Timmy Brown.

Brown was with the Eagles from 1960–67. He was the first player in NFL history to surpass 2,000 all-purpose yards in a season with 2,306 in 1962 and broke his own record a year later with 2,428. Four years later, Gale Sayers of the Bears broke the record with 2,440.

When Brown retired, he had 12,684 all-purpose yards, fourth highest at the time behind only Jim Brown, Bobby Mitchell, and Ollie Matson, all Hall of Famers.

Timmy Brown hauls in a pass against the New Orleans Saints in 1967. *AP Photo/Bill Ingraham.*

Brown had joined the Eagles in 1960 and was a part of a championship team as a rookie. He was one of the greatest running backs in Eagles history, who could catch passes and also return punts and kickoffs. Brown was second in club history in rushing yards (3,703) and rushing touchdowns (29) behind only Steve Van Buren and he was second in all-purpose yards behind Pete Retzlaff (7,049) at the time he was traded to Baltimore in 1968.

13 Four: Jerry Williams, 1953–54; Ed Khayat, 1958–61 and 1964–65; Marion Campbell, 1956–61; and Doug Pederson, 1999.

Williams stood out on offense for the Eagles as a halfback and a receiver for two years, yet when he started his coaching career, he coached defense. Williams was in charge of the Eagles defense in 1960 when they won the NFL championship. Khayat had two tours of duty with the Eagles as a defensive tackle and played alongside Marion Campbell for four years. When Andy Reid took over the Eagles in 1999, he bought in Pederson, drafted Donovan McNabb, and sent Bobby Hoying and Rodney Peete away in trades.

At one time, all four were assistant coaches with the Eagles, and they also each played for NFL championship teams. Williams was with the Los Angeles Rams in 1951 when they beat Cleveland. Campbell and Khayat were part of the 1960 Eagles who beat Green Bay, and Pederson was with the Packers when they won the Super Bowl over New England after the 1996 season.

14 Dick Vermeil.

He had started his professional coaching career as an assistant with the Los Angeles Rams in 1969. George Allen hired

Dick Vermeil yells from the sideline during his rookie season coaching the Eagles in 1976. *AP Photo.*

Vermeil as the first full-time special teams coach in the NFL. Vermeil won the Super Bowl with the St. Louis Rams in 1999. After Vermeil retired from the Eagles after the 1982 season, many wondered whether he would come back and coach again. He was broadcasting NFL and college games on TV, but the Rams lured out of retirement.

Over the fourteen years Vermeil was away from coaching, he was often rumored to be in the running for open coaching jobs. He was rumored to be coming back to the Eagles, but it never happened and it was just as well. Oftentimes when a coach comes back to his former team, he is usually not as successful the second time around. Joe Gibbs returned to Washington and made it to the playoffs once in four years and had a losing record, while Bud Grant returned to Minnesota and had one losing season and stepped away for good.

In his third year with the Rams, Vermeil won the Super Bowl over the Tennessee Titans, coached by Jeff Fisher, another former Eagles assistant coach. The Titans got down to the 1-yard line when time ran out in one of the best and most exciting Super Bowls.

15 Doug Pederson in 2016.

Nick Skorich had been the first Eagles coach to win his first two games in 1961. The defending NFL champions started off by beating Cleveland, 27–20, and Washington, 14–7, at Franklin Field, but fell to the Cardinals a week later at home, 30–27. They finished 10–4, but missed winning the Eastern Conference by a half-game.

The Eagles began the 2016 season under rookie coach Pederson with a 29–10 victory over Cleveland at the Linc. Unlike Skorich, Pederson was taking over a team that had a losing season the year before. The following week at Chicago, the Eagles beat the Bears at Soldier Field, 29–14, as Pederson matched Skorich. Returning back home the following week, the Eagles made it three straight with a 34–3 win over Pittsburgh. The streak ended in the fourth game when the Eagles fell to the Lions in Detroit, 24–23.

The Eagles went 7–9 in Pederson's first year. After a 3–0 start, they fell to 5–9, with two losses by one point and two others by five points. The Eagles rebounded to win their final two games.

16 Greasy Neale.

He coached the Eagles from 1941 to 1950, winning consecutive NFL championships in 1948 and 1949. He was let go two months after the 1950 season. This was the beginning of the Eagles' downfall in the 1950s. At the time, Neale had the most wins by an Eagles coach, 66 (including postseason), and is the only Eagles coach to have seven straight winning seasons.

Before coaching the Eagles, Neale spent eight years playing major league baseball, including 22 games with the Phillies in 1921. He was a member of the Cincinnati Reds in 1919 when they won the World Series over the Chicago White Sox, five games to three. This was the second of four years that the World Series was a best five of nine. He was Cincinnati's leading hitter in the Series at .357. That World Series was allegedly fixed by seven White Sox players, and an eighth supposedly knew about it, but didn't report it. Although they weren't found guilty, Commissioner Kenesaw Mountain Landis banned all eight for life.

17 Jerry Williams.

Pete Retzlaff remembered that Williams had used the five-man defensive backfield in a 1961 game against the Chicago Bears. "Prevent was the concept," said Pete. "Basically, it was designed to stop the passing attack at that time of teams that had outstanding receivers. We always felt that when their offense was balanced in favor of the passing game, we would do something to try to throttle that, then maybe we could handle the run. So Jerry actually introduced the five defensive back defense by taking out either a lineman or linebacker. In our case, we started by taking out a linebacker. It turned out to be a halfway decent defense that could be used at any time during crucial passing situations, especially third or second and long.

"Jerry used it in the 1961 Bears game. We were successful with it and at that time, Chicago had an assistant coach, George Allen, and, following the game, Allen asked Jerry how he programmed or patterned that defense. What responsibility he has assigned to each individual, and Jerry sat down and went over it with him and the rest is history. Allen went on to become the head coach of the Rams where he put that defense to work, called it the nickel defense, which was a catchy phrase. And it caught on. Of course, George Allen, I think is acknowledged receiving credit for installing that defense, but it started right here in Philadelphia with Jerry Williams."

18 Joe Kuharich coached the Eagles from 1964 to 1968. It was not a popular move when new owner Jerry Wolman hired Kuharich. He had coached two teams in the NFL, the Chicago Cardinals and the Washington Redskins, and had losing records with both. Kuharich then switched over to college football and was the head coach at Notre Dame for four years and is still the only coach at Notre Dame with a losing record.

When Wolman was searching for a coach, Paul Brown, who had built a dynasty in Cleveland but had been let go after the 1962 season, was available. There was an assistant coach with the Chicago Bears, George Allen, whose defense had a lot to do with the team winning the 1963 NFL championship. After the game when Chicago beat the New York Giants at Wrigley Field, Allen was presented with the game ball. Many were hoping that Norm Van Brocklin would leave Minnesota and come back to Philadelphia. Van Brocklin said that when he was traded to Philadelphia, where he really didn't want to come to in the first place, he thought he would be the next coach when Buck Shaw stepped down.

When the Eagles won the title, Shaw retired. What better way to bow out then with a champion? Van Brocklin also retired. He was offered a position as a playing assistant coach which he turned down right away. Nick Skorich was hired to replace Shaw but lasted only three seasons, going 15–24–3. Wolman took it upon himself to put Kuharich in charge even though Vince McNally was still general manager. Kuharich promptly traded off two future Hall of Famers, Sonny Jurgensen and Tommy McDonald. Before the season, McNally resigned and Kuharich was named general manager and, after his first season, received a fifteen-year contract. Kuharich began his tenure with a 6–8 record in 1964 and finished it by going 2–12 in 1968. He had one winning season and was fired when Leonard Tose purchased the team on May 1, 1969. His overall record with the Eagles was 28–41–1.

19 Vince Lombardi.

He had never been a professional head coach. He coached under Red Blaik at Army for five years and was the New York Giants offensive coordinator for five years. "I had a little problem," McNally recalled. "Mr. (Frank) McNamee was the president of the ball club, and when you go after another coach, an assistant coach, you go through the proper channels and call the club up and say, 'Would you give me permission to talk to Vince Lombardi?' They always do. They never turn you down. Mr. McNamee came in and said, 'I never told you to do anything that you didn't want to do, but I am asking you personally. Do this as a favor. Call up Lombardi yourself and don't go through the proper channels.' I said I don't know how this is going to come out but I think we should do it the other way around. So I called up Vince and he came down to Philadelphia and we sat in the 30th Street train station for about three or four hours and we ironed everything out. We had a handshake and I told him that I could give him a one-year contract and after the first year was over, he would be the boss, and he could come in and talk to me and we would work things out with an extended contract and more money and more everything.

"So Vince said to me, 'I have to go back and talk to the Maras [the Giants owners], and the Maras and Lombardi were like father and son. They were very close. He didn't want to do anything to hurt them. So he said, 'I'll go back and talk to them and tell them what we talked about.' Lombardi said he would call me at six o'clock, and he called me and he said he was sorry but he was going to stay right here in New York."

20 Mike Ditka, Bill Cowher, and Doug Pederson.

Ditka played with the Eagles in 1967 and 1968 and was the coach of the Chicago Bears in 1985 when they went 15–1 and beat New England, 46–10, in the Super Bowl. Ditka took over as the Eagles tight end after Pete Retzlaff retired. He played with the Bears when they won the NFL championship in 1963 and later played on the Cowboys Super Bowl-winning team in 1971. Ditka retired after the 1972 season and stayed with Dallas for nine years as an assistant coach under Tom Landry. The call to come to Chicago came from the founder of the Bears, Ditka's former coach, George Halas, in 1982.

Cowher was a linebacker for the Eagles in 1983 and 1984. After he retired, he spent four years with Cleveland and three years with Kansas City as an assistant coach before he became the head coach of the Pittsburgh Steelers in 1992. He had a tough act to follow. Chuck Noll had retired after 23 years in which he became the first coach to win four Super Bowls. Cowher stayed with the Steelers for 15 years, won eight division titles, made the playoffs 10 times, and won the Super Bowl by defeating Seattle, 21–10, in 2006.

Andy Reid bought Doug Pederson to Philadelphia in 1999 after being his quarterbacks coach in Green Bay.

Pederson played in all 16 games and was the starter for the first nine games until Donovan McNabb, who was drafted with the second pick in the first round, took over as the starter. Pederson stayed with the Eagles for one year. After retiring as a player at the conclusion of the 2004 season, Pederson started coaching in high school until Reid bought him to the Eagles staff beginning in 2009. He stayed for four years until Reid left the Eagles and took over in Kansas City. Pederson followed him to the Chiefs and was the offensive coordinator for three seasons, before becoming the head coach of the Eagles in 2016.

Winning Super Bowls with other teams before being with the Eagles wasn't just limited to former players. Four former assistant coaches won Super Bowls: Jon Gruden, Tom Coughlin, Sean Payton, and John Harbaugh.

Jon Gruden won with Tampa Bay in 2003 after defeating the Eagles, 27–10, for the NFC championship in the last game ever played at the Vet. Tampa Bay beat Oakland, Gruden's former team, in the Super Bowl, 48–21.

Tom Coughlin won Super Bowls with the New York Giants in 2008 and 2012. Both times, they beat New England late in the game. The first time, the Giants scored the winning touchdown with 35 seconds to go when Eli Manning threw a 35-yard touchdown pass to Plaxico Burress, ending the Patriots' shot at becoming the first NFL team to go 19–0, 17–14. The second time, New York rallied and won the game with 57 seconds to play, 21–17, when Ahmad Bradshaw scored on a 6-yard run.

Sean Payton won when New Orleans defeated Indianapolis, 31–17, in 2010, giving the Colts the distinction of being the second NFL club (the Los Angeles/St. Louis Rams were the first) to lose Super Bowls representing two different cities. They lost as the Baltimore Colts in 1969.

John Harbaugh won with Baltimore Ravens in 2012, defeating the San Francisco 49ers, 34–31. The Ravens were coached by his younger brother, Jim, marking the only time that brothers coached against each other in the Super Bowl. The 49ers were attempting to become the second team to win six Super Bowls.

Four former assistant coaches with the Eagles coached teams that lost the Super Bowl: John Rauch, Marv Levy, Jeff Fisher, and Ron Rivera.

John Rauch was coaching Oakland when they lost to Green Bay, 33–14, in Super Bowl II in 1968. He became an assistant coach with the Eagles after leaving the Raiders the following year.

Marv Levy lost four Super Bowls with Buffalo from 1991 to 1994, becoming the second coach to lose four Super Bowls but the first to lose four straight. His first loss was to the Giants when Scott Norwood missed a 47-yard field goal attempt with four seconds remaining. The next loss was to Washington, 37–24, and Dallas took out the Bills in the next two Super Bowls, 52–17 and 30–13.

Jeff Fisher lost with Tennessee, 23–16, in 2000 to the Dick Vermeil's Rams team although the Titans got to within a foot of the goal line on the last play of the game.

Ron Rivera was the most recent with Carolina in 2016, falling to Denver, 24–10. The Broncos led all the way in winning their third Super Bowl.

21 Buddy Ryan was famous for his colorful quotes when he was the defensive coordinator for the Chicago Bears. He called William Perry, known as "the Refrigerator," a wasted draft pick. He didn't change his ways upon becoming the coach of the Eagles. Ryan was never afraid to express his opinion.

1. b, Cris "All he does is catch touchdown passes" Carter
2. d, Michael "He looks like a reject guard out of the USFL" Haddix
3. e, Keith "A medical reject" Byars
4. c, Earnest "I would trade him for a six-pack that doesn't have to be cold" Jackson
5. a, Luis "Why would I try to hurt him?" Zendejas

Carter spent three years with the Eagles before heading to Minnesota after the 1989 season. He was inducted in the Pro Football Hall of Fame in 2013. Haddix had joined the Eagles in 1983 as their first-round pick, and when Ryan took over as coach in 1986, he kept him around for three more years. There was a lot of speculation whether Ryan would take Byars in the first round of the 1986 draft. When the Eagles turn came to make their selection, they took Byars, who ended up playing seven seasons in Philadelphia. Jackson spent only the 1985 season with the Eagles and gained 1,028 yards on the ground, but Ryan sent him packing anyway. Zendejas was in his second season with the Eagles in 1989 when Ryan sent him away. They picked up Roger Ruzek, who had started the 1989 season with Dallas. Zendejas replaced him on the Cowboys and Dallas coach Jimmy Johnson accused Ryan of placing a $200 bounty on his former kicker in their Thanksgiving Day game, won by the Eagles, 27–0.

22 Temple Stadium and Municipal Stadium.

The Eagles lost their first game in Baker Bowl, 25–0, to the Portsmouth Spartans in 1933, and it was also their first night game. The Eagles won their first game at Temple Stadium, 64–0, over Cincinnati in 1934. This is still the largest shutout in the history of the NFL, and the 64 points is still a club record for the most points scored in a game. This was the biggest margin of victory in a regular season NFL game.

When the Eagles moved into Municipal Stadium in 1936, they beat the New York Giants, 10–7, in their opener. After that, it was all losses. First, they lost in 1940 to the New York Giants at Shibe Park, 20–14. In 1958, in their first game at Franklin Field, they were beaten by Washington, 24–14. When the Vet opened in 1971, Dallas, who went on to win the Super Bowl that season, soundly defeated the Eagles, 42–7. After losing their last game at the Vet to Tampa Bay in the NFC Championship Game, which saw the Buccaneers go on and win the Super Bowl, the Eagles drew the Tampaa Bay Buccaneers in the their first game at Lincoln Financial Field in 2003, and they shut out the Eagles, 17–0.

23 Bulldogs, Bell, Stars.

The Continental Football League came to Philadelphia in 1965 and stayed for two years. The Bulldogs were a minor league team and didn't come to Philadelphia to compete with the Eagles. Rather, they were another game in town playing usually on Friday nights at Temple Stadium. They won the 1966 league championship led by quarterback Bob Brodhead, who was Sonny Jurgensen's backup at Duke. Their coach was Wayne Hardin, who had coached Navy for six years, beating Army five times. He had four winning seasons and produced two Heisman and Maxwell Award winners, Joe Bellino in 1960 and Roger Staubach in 1963. The Bulldogs left town after winning the 1966 championship, and Hardin later coached Temple.

The World Football League started play in 1974, and the Philadelphia Bell was a charter member. The Bell was 9–11 in their inaugural season and were 4–7 when the league closed shop the following year.

The United States Football League started play in 1983 and lasted three years. They started their season in the spring and played into July. In 1983, they lost the championship game to Michigan, 24–22, after going 15–3 in the regular season. They won the championship in 1984 when they beat Arizona, 20–3, after going 16–2 in the regular season. In 1985, the team moved to Baltimore and won another championship before the league folded.

24 Nick Foles was selected as the offensive MVP of the 2014 game. He completed 7 of 10 passes for 89 yards and threw a 12-yard touchdown pass to Jordan Cameron, giving Team Sanders (Deion Sanders) a 21–14 lead, but Team Rice (Jerry Rice) came back and won the game, 22–21. Foles had a passer rating of 130.8.

Chuck Bednarik was the first Eagles Pro Bowl MVP in 1954 when he returned an interception 24 yards for a touchdown, recovered a fumble, and punted five times averaging 43 yards.

In 1967, Floyd Peters was the lineman of the game as the East beat the West, 20–10. Reggie White was MVP in 1987 for

Nick Foles thanks the fans after being named the offensive Most Valuable Player of the 2014 NFL Pro Bowl in Honolulu. *AP Photo/Eugene Tanner.*

the NFC who lost the lowest scoring Pro Bowl, 10–6. White recorded four sacks and had seven solo tackles.

Two years later, Randall Cunningham was MVP as the NFC coasted to a 34–3 win over the AFC. Cunningham was 10-for-14 for 63 yards and rushed for 49 yards.

25 Vince Papale.

Papale went to Saint Joseph's on a track scholarship. After graduating from Hawk Hill, he played semi-pro football before spending two years with the Bell in 1974 and 1975. When Dick Vermeil took over as the Eagles coach, he had open tryout camps. Papale went to a tryout camp and made the team in 1976. He was the oldest rookie in the NFL that never played in college outside of kickers. He played from 1976 to 1978 and was voted onto the Eagles 75th Anniversary Team as a special-teams player. He was also a part of the first Eagles team to post a winning season in 1978.

2

SECOND QUARTER
STARTER LEVEL

STARTER LEVEL

(Answers begin on page 47)

The questions in this chapter are devoted to the Eagles' biggest rivals over the years—the Cleveland Browns, Pittsburgh Steelers, New York Giants, and Dallas Cowboys.

1 The Eagles and Browns had a great rivalry beginning in 1950 that ended when the NFL and AFL merged. What was the name of the first league that Cleveland played in?

2 When Cleveland was trying for an undefeated season, the Browns' final game was against the Eagles at Connie Mack Stadium. What year was it?

3 Which two Eagles coaches had the most wins over the Cleveland Browns?
   a. Jim Trimble   b. Buck Shaw
   c. Nick Skorich   d. Andy Reid

4 Who was the first Eagles rookie quarterback to win his first start against Cleveland?

5 In 1960, Chuck Bednarik played both ways in four games. It started in the first game against the Browns. Which injured player did Bednarik replace on defense?

a. Maxie Baughan   b. Tom Brookshier

c. Bob Pellegrini   d. Chuck Weber

6 When the Eagles opened up the 1961 season against the Cleveland Browns at Franklin Field, who returned the opening kickoff 105 yards for a touchdown for the Eagles?

7 When Alexis Thompson bought the Steelers but swapped franchises with the Eagles, who were the Eagles owners?

8 At Forbes Field in 1965, the Eagles tied the NFL record for the most interceptions in a game and most interceptions returned for a touchdown in a game with how many?

9 What was the nickname given to the 1968 Eagles-Steelers game at Pitt Stadium?

10 The Eagles set a club record for the most consecutive wins at home against one team with nine against Green Bay. They tied this record against Pittsburgh. In what year did the Eagles defeat the Steelers for the ninth straight time?

11 What club did the Eagles have the longest winning streak against?

12 When Chuck Bednarik knocked out Frank Gifford at Yankee Stadium in 1960, Gifford fumbled on the play. Which Eagles player recovered the ball assuring the victory?

13 In the first "Miracle at the Meadowlands" at Giants Stadium in 1978, who picked up a fumble and returned it for the winning touchdown?

14 When the Eagles swept the season series with the Giants for the first time in eight years in 1988, the second game was at the Meadowlands. With the game tied, 17–17, in overtime, Luis Zendajas attempted a field goal, but the Giants blocked the kick. Who recovered for the Eagles and returned it 15 yards for the winning touchdown?

15 When the Eagles beat the Giants on their first trip to the new stadium at the Meadowlands in 2010, who returned a punt 65 yards for the game-winning touchdown as time expired?

16 After losing to the Cowboys in Dallas 56–7 in their first meeting of the season in 1966, the Eagles won the rematch at Franklin Field, 24–23. Who set the NFL record in this game for the most kickoffs returned for a touchdown?

17 The Eagles opened the Vet in 1971 against the Dallas Cowboys. Who scored the Eagles' first touchdown there?

18 The Cowboys moved into Texas Stadium during the 1971 season. It wasn't until 1979 that the Eagles beat Dallas there. In that game, who set the club record for the longest field goal?

19 When the Eagles and Dallas first met in a playoff game in the 1980 season, Wilbert Montgomery came within two yards for most yards rushing in a NFC/NFL Championship Game. How many yards did Montgomery rush for?

20 In 1987, Buddy Ryan vowed to get even with Tom Landry after the Cowboys, with some of their top players playing against the Eagles replacement players, won the first meeting. Who scored the touchdown on the last play of the second game between the teams to make the score 37–20?

21 In 1989, the Eagles played the Cowboys on Thanksgiving Day, and new Dallas coach Jimmy Johnson accused Buddy Ryan of putting a bounty on the Cowboys placekicker who had been with the Eagles earlier in the season. Who was the Dallas kicker?

22 In 1995 at Veterans Stadium, the Cowboys were facing a 4th-and-1 at their own 29-yard line late in the fourth quarter. What running back did the Eagles stop twice?

23 In 1997, the Eagles were trailing the Cowboys at Texas Stadium, 21–20, on *Monday Night Football* with four seconds to go. Chris Boniol was getting ready to attempt a 22-yard field goal but the snap was fumbled by what player?

24 When the Eagles started their second season under Andy Reid in 2000 in Dallas, how did the game begin?

25 Who did the Eagles pick up as a free agent from the Cowboys after he led the league in rushing?

STARTER LEVEL
ANSWERS

1 All-America Football Conference.

When World War II ended, the NFL found itself with a rival league in time for the 1946 season. The All-America Football Conference (AAFC) was founded by Arch Ward, sports editor of the *Chicago Tribune*. Before he founded the AAFC, Ward created the baseball All-Star Game in 1933. A year later, he intitated the Chicago College All-Star Game which matched the NFL Champions from the year before against the top players in college football.

There had been three earlier leagues, all of which failed. The AAFC had eight teams in 1946. The Eastern Division had the Brooklyn Dodgers, Buffalo Bisons, Miami Seahawks, and New York Yankees. The Western Division included the Chicago Rockets, Cleveland Browns, Los Angeles Dons, and the San Francisco 49ers. In 1947 and 1948, the Baltimore Colts replaced Miami. The final year, the Dodgers and Yankees merged.

When NFL Commissioner Elmer Layden heard the AAFC was starting in 1946, he was asked for his reaction and he said, "Tell them to get a football first." One team that got a football was the Cleveland Browns and they showed everyone how to use it.

By 1949, the AAFC was struggling. Part of the problem was the Browns were dominating. They won all four championships and were 47–4–3 in the regular season and 5–0 in the postseason. Two of their four regular season losses came against San Francisco who was coached by Buck Shaw and who led the Eagles to the NFL championship in 1960.

Toward the end of the 1949 season, NFL commissioner Bert Bell announced that Baltimore, Cleveland, and San Francisco would join the league in 1950. Otto Graham won the Washington Touchdown Club Player of the Year in 1949 in the AAFC and at the awards ceremony mentioned to George Marshall, the owner of the Washington Redskins, that he might want to hang onto his laundry business now that the Browns were joining the NFL. Marshall responded by telling Graham that he might need a job driving one of his trucks. It turned out that in Graham's six years in the NFL the Browns were were 58–13–1 and beat Washington ten times in eleven games. Cleveland played for the NFL championship all six years and won the title three times.

When the NFL made out its schedule for 1950, the Eagles, who were the 1949 NFL champions, and the Browns, who were the 1949 AAFC champs, were scheduled to meet in the first game of the season. In a way, you could say this was the first Super Bowl, although it was a shame that the two teams didn't meet at the end of 1949 season.

With the Phillies and A's still playing at Shibe Park, the game was moved to Municipal Stadium and 71,237 came to see this historic meeting. Many, including Eagles coach Greasy Neale, thought that the Browns were nothing more than a minor league team. The Eagles knew nothing about Cleveland. Meantime, the Browns, who knew the day was coming when they would join the NFL, had been scouting the Eagles and had a pretty good book on the team.

Cleveland came away with an easy 35–10 win, although several Eagles players including Steve Van Buren were hurt and didn't play. Before the season, Paul Brown had added some players from teams that had folded from the AAFC. Still, the rivalry was on. The two teams played in the same conference, and the Browns swept the season series the first two seasons. Cleveland won its first NFL championship in 1950.

2 In 1953, the Browns were trying to become the first NFL team to go undefeated since the Chicago Bears went 11-0 during the 1942 regular season. Washington stopped them in the NFL Championship Game that year, 14–6. The Browns had won 11 in a row including an early season 37–13 win over the Eagles in Cleveland. The Eagles had failed in their first three meetings to beat the Browns in Philadelphia.

The Eagles went over 40 points for the third time that season in their last game of the season as they beat the Browns, 42–27, at Connie Mack Stadium. The Eagles were trailing, 20–14, in the third quarter when they scored 28 straight points, 14 in the third quarter and 14 in the fourth. Bobby Thomason had a big game, completing 23 of 35 passes and became the first Eagles quarterback to pass for over 300 yards in game against Cleveland. He threw for 331 yards, including three touchdown passes to Pete Pihos (15 yards), Toy Ledbetter (14 yards), and Bobby Walston (17 yards). This was the third game that Thomason passed for 300 or more yards in a game that season, a club record at the time. Thomason's record held up until 1961 when Sonny Jurgensen did it five times.

The Browns next played in the NFL Championship Game against the Lions at Briggs Stadium and once again, the Lions, won, 17–16.

3 a, Jim Trimble and d, Andy Reid with four victories.

Trimble coached the Eagles for four years and beat them once a year, three at home (1953 to 1955) and once on the road in 1952.

The Browns were out of the league for three years when the owner, Art Modell, moved the team to Baltimore in 1996, but the team wasn't going to be the Baltimore Browns, rather the Baltimore Ravens. Cleveland got a new team in 1999, and the Eagles met the Browns every four years beginning in 2000 and Reid's teams won all four, with three being in Cleveland.

Doug Pederson won his first game as an NFL coach when the Eagles beat the Browns, 29–10, in the 2016 opener. This made it five straight wins over the Browns, their longest winning streak over Cleveland. The rivalry with the Browns ended close to fifty years ago, but for twenty years, it was one of the club's biggest.

Andy Reid is one of two Eagles coaches to beat the Cleveland Browns four times. *AP Photo/Chris Gardner.*

4 Sonny Jurgensen.

The Eagles started the 1957 season with three straight losses. The third game was against the Browns in Cleveland. For some reason or other, the schedule makers had the Eagles meeting Cleveland back-to-back. The Browns had their first losing season in 1956 since they joined the NFL. They had won three NFL championships and played for three more, but Otto Graham retired and Cleveland had a bad season. The Browns came to Philadelphia the following Sunday and Hugh Devore, who was in his second and final season coaching the Eagles, benched Bobby Thomason, who was in his sixth and final year with the team. He gave the start to Jurgensen over Al Dorow, who was the third-string quarterback. Jurgensen, who had been taken in the fourth round of that year's NFL draft, led the Eagles to a 17–7 victory. Jurgensen threw his first touchdown pass to Rocky Ryan and scored on a quarterback sneak.

5 Bob Pellegrini.

When the Eagles started the 1960 season by being soundly beaten by Cleveland, 41–27, at Franklin Field, nobody was thinking about the Eagles winning their first NFL championship in eleven years. The Eagles went to Cleveland four weeks later. The Browns were 3–0, followed by the Giants, who were 3–0–1, and the 3–1 Eagles. This meeting was the first of four times that Chuck Bednarik played both ways.

"I had been playing offense all year, and I have no idea whatsoever the defense is all about," remembered Bednarik. "You have offensive meetings and defensive meetings and you go in separate rooms. Early in the game, Bob Pellegrini gets hurt and I am sitting on the bench and I can still picture Buck Shaw yelling, 'Chuck, Chuck. Get in there for Pellegrini.' I didn't know what to do. So I go in there and Chuck Weber was our middle linebacker and I told him, 'Just let me know what I do on a pass. Is it man-to-man or zone?' If it is a run, you just make the tackle."

The Eagles came back from a 22–7 deficit and won the game, 31–29, when Bobby Walston kicked a 38-yard field goal with 10 seconds to go. The win put the Eagles in second place behind the Giants, and two weeks later, the Eagles moved into first place to stay. "You could call that game a turning point," said Pete Retzlaff, "or a momentum gathering situation. But psychologically, as a result, we were sure then we could go all the way. And we also realized that with a little extra effort, you can make the breaks go your way. People will say that Walston was lucky to kick that field goal with ten seconds to go. Every team that has won the championship as a result of their hustle and mental outlook and their approach during that season, they have always made the breaks bounce their way."

6 Timmy Brown.

With both the Browns and Giants looking to dethrone the Eagles as NFL champs in 1961, the Eagles met Cleveland on Opening Day at Franklin Field and the season got off to a great beginning. For starters, Brown returned the opening kickoff 105 yards for a touchdown, a club record at the time. The Eagles went on and beat Cleveland, 27–20, but the season ended on a down note as the Giants won the Eastern Conference, and the Browns finished behind the Eagles. This was the last time that the Browns finished behind the Eagles.

For the rest of the decade, the Browns dominated the Eagles. Beginning in 1967, the two conferences were each divided up into two divisions setting up an extra round of playoffs. The Eagles and Browns were put in separate divisions and the two teams met only once a year until the merger in 1970.

From 1950 to 1966, the only team in their conference they never swept was Cleveland. The closest they came was in 1962 when they beat the Browns at Franklin Field, 35–7, but they tied at Cleveland, 14–14.

The Browns swept the Eagles eight times in seventeen years including three straight beginning in 1963.

When it was announced that Cleveland was switching over to the American Football Conference, this ended the rivalry between the two teams. It was sad not to see the Eagles and Cleveland going at it like the old days even though the Browns held the series lead, 26–10–1. The Eagles fared better against the Browns after the merger.

Since 1970, the two teams faced each other twelve times with the Eagles winning seven, including the last five. Carson Wentz was drafted in 2016 and the following September, made his NFL debut and became the second Eagles rookie quarterback to beat the Browns in his first NFL start.

7 Bert Bell and Art Rooney.

The Eagles were one of three new teams that came into the National Football League in 1933. Future NFL commissioner Bell and Lud Gray were the original owners. Philadelphia had the Frankford Yellow Jackets from 1924 to 1931. The Pennsylvania Blue Laws had been changed, allowing professional sports to be played on Sunday.

Pittsburgh started out with the nickname Pirates like their counterparts in baseball and didn't change their name until 1941. After the 1940 season, Rooney sold his club to Alexis Thompson, and Rooney purchased half of the Eagles. Before the 1941 season began, Bell and Rooney swapped franchises with Thompson, whose first move was to bring in Greasy Neale as his coach, and the Eagles rose to prominence in the decade.

During World War II, players in all sports were going into the service. The Eagles and Steelers decided to merge in June for the 1943 season and were called the Steagles. This arrangement lasted one year and the team went 5–4–1. They finished a game behind Washington and the New York Giants, who tied for first place. The Redskins met the Giants in a play-off game which Washington won, but they fell to the Chicago Bears in the NFL Championship Game. The Steagles had six home games, four at Shibe Park and two at Forbes Field. Bill Hewitt, who made the All-Decade team of the 1930s and had played with the Eagles from 1937 to 1939, came out of retirement to play for the team.

Greasy Neale and Walt Kiesling were the co-coaches. Other franchises were affected by the war that season. The Cleveland Rams suspended operations, but Boston was granted a team beginning in 1944.

This was also the first time the Eagles had a winning season, the first of seven straight in the decade. The following season, the Eagles went back to being the Eagles, and the Steelers merged with the Chicago Cardinals and won only one game.

Cleveland resumed operations and Boston joined the NFL, but the Brooklyn Tigers folded at the end of the season.

8 Nine interceptions, three returned for touchdowns.

The Steelers beat the Eagles at Franklin Field in 1965, 20–14, for their most recent win in Philadelphia but when the two teams met in the next to last game of the season at Pitt Stadium, the Eagles came out on top, 47–13. In that game, the Eagles tied an NFL record for the most interceptions in a game with nine and also tied the NFL record which has since been broken for most touchdowns scored on interceptions in a game with three. This broke the club record which the Eagles set in 1950 with eight when they beat the Chicago Cardinals in Comiskey Park. The 47 points was the most the Eagles ever scored in a game against the Steelers.

Jim Nettles intercepted three passes, Joe Scarpati two, while Maxie Baughan, Irv Cross, Nate Ramsey, and George Tarasovic each had one as Tommy Wade threw seven interceptions and Bill Nelsen threw two. Baughan (33 yards), Nettles (56), and Tarasovic (40) scored touchdowns. The offense put 20 points on the board in the first quarter before Baughan brought the first interception back for a touchdown as the Eagles took a 27–0 lead after the first 15 minutes. Nettles took his interception back for six points in the second quarter, and Tarasovic scored in the third quarter. Tarasovic, a defensive end, was with the Eagles for three seasons, and this was his only interception. The Eagles also tied their club record by forcing 12 turnovers.

The Eagles and Steelers battled each other twice each year from the end of World War II through 1966. The Eagles swept the Steelers ten times and got swept only four times. Pittsburgh came close to winning the Eastern Conference in 1963. The Eagles and the Steelers met each other twice that year and both games ended in a tie. The second tie was the last game the Steelers played at Forbes Field. They moved their games to Pitt Stadium in 1964 and moved into Three Rivers Stadium in 1970.

9 The "O. J. Bowl."

By 1968, the Eagles and Steelers were meeting once a year instead of twice. This was one season they didn't want bragging rights in Pennsylvania. In 1968, both teams were 0–6 when they met at Pitt Stadium. The game was known as the "O. J. Bowl" since everyone figured one of these two teams would get to draft running back O. J. Simpson from Southern California. The Steelers won the game, 6–3. Booth Lusteg kicked two fourth-quarter field goals and Eagles fans were happy about that. Then to make things better, the Steelers beat the Falcons the following week, 41–21. Buffalo was 1–6–1, Atlanta, 1–6, and the Eagles were in the drivers' seat to get the number one draft pick. Then a strange thing happened. After starting the season with 11 consecutive losses, the Eagles won their next two games, over Detroit on Thanksgiving Day, 12–0, on four Sam Baker field goals and then New Orleans at Franklin Field, 29–17. Goodbye to the number one draft choice.

When the season ended, neither the Eagles nor Steelers had a chance to get Simpson as it turned out. The Bills, with a 1–12–1 record, picked first in the draft and took Simpson. The Falcons, who were 2–12, picked next and took George Kunz, an offensive tackle from Notre Dame. The Eagles, with Kuharich still making the calls, took Leroy Keyes, a running back from Purdue who eventually was converted to a defensive back, and the Steelers selected Joe Greene. Nobody knew it at the time but great days for the Steelers were around the corner when they took Greene.

As part of the AFL-NFL merger, the Steelers moved over to the AFC and became the team of the 1970s, winning four

Super Bowls. Pittsburgh has won two more Super Bowls since then while the Eagles are still looking for their first.

10 2016.

When the 2016 season rolled around, the Steelers made their first trip back to Philadelphia in eight years, and the Eagles made it nine straight home victories over Pittsburgh which tied the club record for most consecutive wins at home against one team. Earlier, the Eagles had knocked off Green Bay nine straight between 1974 and 2006.

Since the merger in 1970, the Steelers have returned to Philadelphia six times and lost each time. The Eagles went back across the state six times to meet the Steelers and won twice. When Doug Pederson became the first coach in club history to win his first three games in 2016, he did it against the Steelers in a 34–3 win with rookie quarterback Carson Wentz at the helm. Wentz became the second Eagles rookie quarterback to win his first three starts, but the first to do it starting a season. The Eagles had taken a 13–3 lead at half-time, and with 2:06 gone in the third quarter, Wentz threw a 73-yard touchdown pass to Darren Sproles. Wentz was 23 of 31 and threw for 301 yards.

11 The New York Giants, twelve games.

The Eagles started the streak in 1975 at Shea Stadium and made it twelve straight in 1981 at Giants Stadium. The Eagles have met the Giants 166 times in the regular season, the most of any opponent. New York leads the series, 84–80–2. The teams have split four postseason contests.

The Eagles traveled to New York for their first game in the NFL and were beaten by the Giants, 56–0, at the Polo Grounds in 1933. In the first 22 meetings between the two teams, the Eagles won only four times. When Greasy Neale started to build powerhouse teams for the second half of the decade in 1944, the Eagles turned things around. They captured nine and lost only two with one tie. The Eagles had three straight sweeps over the Giants beginning in 1947 as they advanced to the NFL Championship Game that season and won it in 1948 and 1949 after losing the 1947 title game.

The Giants snapped their twelve-game losing streak in 1981, 20–10, and proved it was no fluke when the two teams met again at the Vet in the Wild Card Game and New York won once again, 27–21.

12 Chuck Weber.

The Giants played their home games at the Polo Grounds from 1925 through 1955. They switched to Yankee Stadium in 1956, but it wasn't until 1960 that the Eagles knocked off the Giants at "The House That Ruth Built." When they did, it came in one of the most famous games between the two teams as the Eagles rallied from a 10–0 deficit in the second half and won, 17–10, as Chuck Bednarik knocked out Giants star Frank Gifford. With the game tied, 10–10, Bednarik caused Mel Triplett to fumble, and Jimmy Carr picked up the loose ball, returning it 38 yards for a touchdown as the Eagles took the lead for good. Bednarik had played only defense in the first half, but in the second half, he went back to offensive center and played both ways for the second time that season. The Giants had one last chance when Gifford caught a pass but was hit by Bednarik and fumbled the ball. Chuck Weber recovered the loose ball. A picture showed Bednarik excited about Weber recovering the fumble, unaware that Gifford was knocked out and had to be

Chuck Weber recovers Frank Gifford's fumble after he was hit by Chuck Bednarik (60) in a key 1960 game. *AP Photo.*

taken off the field on a stretcher. Gifford not only missed the last four games, but he sat out the 1961 season before returning in 1962 for three more years. It was also the Eagles' first win over New York on the road since 1952.

At one time, the Eagles and Giants met three times a year starting with a preseason game at Princeton. The Eagles and Giants met thirteen straight years at Palmer Stadium from 1962 to 1974. Each team won six games and one ended in a tie.

Yankee Stadium was going to be shut down after the Yankees completed their 1973 season, and it wouldn't reopen until 1976. The Giants played their first two home games of the year at Yankee Stadium, the second a 23–23 tie with the Eagles. Harold Carmichael scored the last touchdown on a 16-yard touchdown pass from Roman Gabriel. The Giants tied the game when Pete Gogolak kicked a 14-yard field goal as time expired.

The Giants never returned to Yankee Stadium. They finished the 1973 season at the Yale Bowl in New Haven, Connecticut, and played there in 1974. A year later, they moved into Shea Stadium and to Giants Stadium when it was completed in 1976.

The two teams met once at the Yale Bowl and once at Shea Stadium, and both times the Eagles came away with a win.

13 Herman Edwards.

The Eagles won their first six meetings at Giants Stadium but it was the third game that the Eagles won in 1978 that was the most memorable. With time running out, New York led, 17–12. The Eagles were out of timeouts and all the Giants had to do was kneel down and let the clock run out, but instead quarterback Joe Pisarcik tried to hand the ball off to Larry Csonka and the play got botched. Edwards picked up the loose ball on the 26-yard line and took it in for a game-winning touchdown with 20 seconds left.

Broadcaster Merrill Reese described the play:

"Under 30 seconds left in the game. Pisarcik fumbles the football. It is picked up by Edwards. 15, 10, 5, touchdown Eagles. I don't believe it. I don't believe it. I don't believe what has occurred here, ladies and gentlemen. As Pisarcik came forward, he fumbled the football. Charlie Johnson hit him and Herman Edwards picked it up and ran it in for a touchdown."

It was the Eagles' sixth of twelve straight straight wins over the Giants and helped make it possible for them to qualify for the postseason for the first time since 1960, where they dropped a 14–13 heartbreaker at Atlanta in the Wild Card Game.

14 Clyde Simmons.

Lawrence Taylor blocked Luis Zendejas's 30-yard field goal attempt, but Simmons grabbed the ball and took it 15 yards into the end zone to win the game, 23–17. Simmons saved the game a week earlier in Pittsburgh when he blocked Gary Anderson's 57-yard field goal attempt on the last play of the game. This was the first time that a blocked field goal by the Eagles turned into a touchdown. Simmons, who played eight seasons with the Eagles, finished third in career sacks. Simmons also had 19 sacks in 1992, second best in club history for one season.

The win also put the Eagles into a three-way tie for first place with the Giants and the Cardinals. The Eagles went on and won three of their last four games to win the NFC East title for the first time since 1980. Not only did they win their division, they received a bye in the first round of the playoffs for the first time in eight years and a trip to Chicago where Buddy Ryan had been the defensive coordinator when the 1985 Bears won the Super Bowl. Chicago hung on in the fog in the second half and won the game, 20–12.

15 DeSean Jackson.

It took only three years for the Eagles to pull off a "miracle" at the first Meadowlands stadium and only one game at MetLife Stadium when it opened in 2010. With both teams at 9–4, the Giants were up, 31–10. Michael Vick got things rolling in the fourth quarter, throwing two touchdown passes and scoring one to tie the game, 31–31. Time was running out. All the Giants had to do was punt the ball out of bounds and go to overtime. Instead, punter Matt Dodge kept the ball in play and Jackson returned the punt 65 yards for a touchdown. This was the first game in NFL history when the winning touchdown was scored on a punt return as time expired. The Eagles tied the club record for scoring the most points in the fourth quarter with 28 and the win put the Eagles into first place to stay. Broadcasters Merrill Reese and Mike Quick described Jackson's winning touchdown:

REESE: Fourteen seconds to go, 31–31. Matt Dodge to punt, gets a high snap, gets it away, it's a knuckler. Jackson takes it at the 35, fumbles it, picks it up, looks for running room. He's at the 40, he's at the 45, midfield . . .
QUICK: OH!

REESE: He's at the 40.
QUICK: OH!

REESE: He's going to go. DeSean Jackson!
QUICK: OH!

REESE: I don't care if he jumps, dives, he's running around and he's in the end zone, and there's no time and the Eagles win! The Eagles win!

DeSean Jackson caps a remarkable Eagles comeback with a 65-yard punt return on the final play of the game, giving them a 38–31 victory over the New York Giants in the second "Miracle at the Meadowlands." *AP Photo/Bill Kostroun.*

QUICK: This is Miracle at the Meadowlands Number Two! Miracle in the New Meadowlands, baby.

When the season ended, the Eagles and Giants were tied for first place, but the Eagles won the tiebreaker on the virtue of having swept New York that season. Green Bay eliminated the Eagles from the playoffs at Lincoln Financial Field and went on to win the Super Bowl.

16 Timmy Brown.

The Cowboys entered the NFL in 1960. Dallas, which had NFL football with the Texans in 1952, all of sudden had two teams, and both played at the Cotton Bowl. The AFL was born that year, and Dallas was one of the eight teams.

The Cowboys hadn't had a winning season in their first six years in the NFL. But when they got good, they got great beginning in 1966. They made the playoffs for the next eight years. In an early season meeting with the Eagles at the Cotton Bowl, Dallas trounced the Eagles, 56–7, running up the score. With 22 seconds left in the game, Les Shy ran it in for a touchdown from the 1-yard line. The 56 points was a Dallas club record at the time for the most points scored in a game. The rivalry was underway.

The two teams met at Franklin Field four weeks later, and the Eagles not only beat the Cowboys, they did it in the one of the strangest games in NFL history. Brown set an NFL record by returning two kickoffs for touchdowns of 93 and 90 yards and Aaron Martin returned a punt 67 yards for a touchdown. Sam Baker added a field goal. Late in the game, the Cowboys were driving when Dan Reeves had the ball stripped from him on the 13-yard line by Joe Scarpati, assuring the Eagles the victory.

The following season, Brown had his jaw broken by Lee Roy Jordan in the next-to-last-game of the season. This added more fuel to the rivalry. It turned out to be the last game that Brown played with the Eagles. He was traded to the Baltimore Colts for Alvin Haymond and was with them when they lost Super Bowl III to the Jets.

Whether both teams are good or both teams are bad, or if one is good and the other isn't, it is the Dallas games that are always talked about.

17 Al Nelson.

The Eagles played their first game at Veterans Stadium in 1971 against Dallas. Trailing 42–0, with less than two minutes to go, Mike Clark, who had been with the Eagles in 1963, attempted a field goal, but Nelson returned it a 101 yards for a touchdown, a club record.

This was the second time that Nelson returned a missed field goal for the Eagles. His first came five years earlier at Franklin Field in a 33–21 win over Cleveland. The Eagles didn't win their first game at the Vet until they beat the Giants in their fourth home game of the season and they had to wait until 1973 before they knocked off Dallas there.

In 1974, the Eagles met the Cowboys for the first time on *Monday Night Football* and Joe Lavender returned a fumble 96 yards for a touchdown at Veterans Stadium. The Eagles won the game, 13–10, as Tom Dempsey kicked a game-winning 45-yard field goal with 25 seconds left. This was the second straight home win over the Cowboys, something that the Eagles hadn't accomplished since 1967 and wouldn't happen again during the regular season until 1988.

The Eagles had to wait until 1980 before they beat Dallas at the Vet again. Tied 10–10 with 4:25 to go in the fourth quarter, the Eagles won the game, 17–10, when Ron Jaworski threw a 15-yard touchdown pass to Charlie Smith.

18 Tony Franklin.

The Eagles hadn't beaten the Cowboys in Dallas since 1965. The Eagles dropped five straight at the Cotton Bowl from 1966 to 1970, and a year later the Cowboys moved into Texas Stadium during the season. The Eagles dropped their first eight in a row in the stadium that featured a hole in its roof.

Franklin booted a 59-yard field goal to help the Eagles beat the Cowboys, 31–21, in their first road appearance on *Monday Night Football*. Tied 7–7 in the second quarter, John Walton put the Eagles ahead for good when he threw a 29-yard touchdown pass to Charlie Smith and Franklin kicked his 59-yard field goal right before the half ended.

The win got the Eagles back on the winning track. They had started 6–1 before dropping three straight. The victory over the Cowboys was the first of five in their final six games of the season to finish 11–5 and a spot in the playoffs. In the next-to-last game of the season, Dallas beat the Eagles, 24–17, to win the NFC East, but the Eagles were assured a wild-card berth. Both teams finished with 11–5 records, but the Cowboys won the division based on a better conference record, 10–2 to 9–3.

19 194 yards.

Philadelphia hadn't been this excited about a football game in the city of Brotherly Love since 1960 when the Eagles defeated the Green Bay Packers, 17–13, to win the NFL title. The Eagles and Cowboys were meeting at the Vet for the NFC championship and a trip to New Orleans for the Super Bowl.

The teams split two meetings in the regular season with the Eagles winning at the Vet, 17–10, and wrapping up the Eastern Division for the first time in 20 years despite a 35–27 loss to the Cowboys at Texas Stadium in the last game of the year. For Dallas to win the division, they had to beat the Eagles by 25 points or more.

As with the Eagles' earlier NFL/NFC championship games in Philadelphia, weather was a big factor. In 1948, the

Eagles beat the Chicago Cardinals in the snow, and twelve years later, they beat the Packers when the temperature started out in the low forties but kept dropping. The temperature was 16 degrees for the Eagles-Cowboys game.

Knowing that the Cowboys had bad luck wearing their blue jerseys, Dick Vermeil said the Eagles would wear their white jerseys. Cowboys president and general manager Tex Schramm wasn't happy about that and said Vermeil had a lot of George Allen in him. Vermeil took that as a compliment because he said Allen, who while with the Rams had given him his first NFL job, was a great coach.

With only 2:11 gone in the first quarter, Wilbert Montgomery scored on a 42-yard run to give the Eagles a 7–0 lead. The Cowboys tied it in the second quarter when Tony Dorsett scored on a 3-yard run. After that, the Cowboys never crossed the Eagles 39-yard line. The Eagles went ahead for good in the third quarter as Tony Franklin kicked a 29-yard field goal and Leroy Harris scored on a nine-yard run. Franklin closed out the scoring with a 20-yard field goal in the fourth quarter. The Eagles picked up 263 yards rushing with Montgomery contributing 194 yards, just two yards short of the record of 196 that Steve Van Buren set in 1949 in the Eagles' 14–0 win over the Rams in the 1949 NFL Championship Game.

Years later, Stan Walters, an offensive tackle who played for the Eagles during Vermeil's era, became a broadcaster alongside Merrill Reese. Walters once had Tex Schramm lined up as a halftime guest. During the first half, Walters remarked that Schramm had the officials in his pocket. There was a knock on

Wilbert Montgomery rushed for 194 yards against the Dallas Cowboys in the 1980 NFC Championship Game. *AP Photo.*

the window of the broadcast booth and Schramm, who was next door, showed his pockets were empty. Needless to say, Schramm passed on doing the interview and Walters had to look for another guest.

20 Keith Byars.

From 1982 to 1985, the rivalry with the Cowboys was kind of quiet until Buddy Ryan arrived in Philadelphia in 1986. The following year, the Eagles, in their first game back after using replacement players for three games during a players' strike, were playing Dallas at the Vet. The entire Eagles team had stayed out on strike while several of the Cowboys players had crossed the picket line and played in those games.

Buddy Ryan let everyone know how he felt about the Cowboys running up the score on his replacement players two weeks earlier, 41–22, and vowed to get even.

With the Eagles comfortably in front late in the fourth quarter, Randall Cunningham had taken a knee and was running out the clock, or so it seemed. Only one more kneel down was needed and the Eagles would have a 30–20 victory. Cunningham took the snap, faked kneeling down, and threw the ball towards the end zone to Mike Quick. Pass interference was called and the Eagles got the ball on the 1-yard line. On the next play, Byars took it into the end zone, making it a 37–20 final. Ryan said, "They started it. We finished it." Ryan went 4–2 against Landry and 8–2 overall against Dallas. As Ryan used to say, "Dallas knows we are going to beat them. They just don't know how." The Eagles swept the Cowboys in 1988. First was a come from behind win at home, 24–23. In the last game of the regular season, the Eagles traveled to Texas Stadium and beat the Cowboys, 23–7.

No one knew it at the time, but this was Tom Landry's last game as coach of Dallas. He tied the NFL record for the most consecutive years (29) coaching the same team. During the offseason, Jerry Jones bought the club, canned Landry, and brought in Jimmy Johnson, who lost four in a row to Ryan's Eagles.

21 Luis Zendejas.

Zendejas had been the kicker for the Eagles for the first eight games of the 1989 season before he was replaced by Roger Ruzek, an ex-Cowboy. In Week Twelve, the Eagles played the Cowboys on Thanksgiving Day for the first time since Dallas began hosting a game on that holiday in 1966. Jimmy Johnson was in his first year as coach of Dallas and he accused Buddy Ryan of putting out a bounty on Zendejas who had been picked up by the Cowboys. Ryan denied the charges saying, "Why would I put out a bounty on a kicker who can't kick?" The Eagles shut out the Cowboys, 27–0, the only time that Dallas was blanked on Thanksgiving Day.

Johnson said after the game, "I have absolutely no respect for the way they played the game. I would have said something to Buddy but he wouldn't stand on the field long enough. He put his big, fat rear end into the dressing room."

Ryan upon hearing what Johnson said, "I resent that. I've been on a diet, lost a couple of pounds. I thought I was looking good."

The teams met again in Philadelphia seventeen days later, and the Eagles defeated Dallas, 20–10. After the game, fans threw snowballs at Johnson, who needed a police escort to get back to the locker room.

22 Emmitt Smith.

The Eagles hadn't beaten Dallas in three seasons. The Cowboys had won seven straight and it looked good for eight

Bill Romanowski (53) celebrates after the Eagles stopped Emmitt Smith on fourth down late in a 1995 game. *AP Photo/Chris Gardner.*

in a row when they took a 17–6 lead at the half. In the third quarter, Ricky Watters scored on a 1-yard run and Rodney Peete completed a pass to Fred Barnett good for two points. The Eagles tied the game, 17–17, in the fourth quarter when Gary Anderson kicked a 38-yard field goal. With a little over two minutes to go, Dallas had the ball on a 4th-and-1 at their own 29-yard line. Barry Switzer, in his second season coaching the Cowboys, decided to go for the first down rather than punt. Troy Aikman handed the ball off to Smith, who rushed for 108 yards on 27 carries, but he was stopped, or so it seemed. The officials ruled that the two-minute warning was sounded, and the play was wiped out. Switzer should have gotten the message that this play wasn't working and punted the ball away. Instead, he called the same play, and the Eagles stopped Smith, only this time the play counted.

Trying the same play twice after the first one doesn't count happened a second time less than a minute later. After stopping Smith twice at the Dallas 29-yard line, the Eagles got the ball back. Gary Anderson booted a field goal from 42 yards out, and it looked like the Eagles had gone ahead. The official, though, hadn't given the signal to start. Anderson had to do it all over again and nailed it again with 1:26 left, and the Eagles held on for a 20–17 win.

23 Tommy Hutton.

Over the years, wins were few and far between for the Eagles at Texas Stadium. With a golden opportunity to beat the Cowboys on the road for the second straight year in 1997, Chris Boniol, in his first year with the Eagles, was getting ready to attempt a game-winning field goal with Philadelphia trailing, 21–20. Hutton, not the slick-fielding first basemen the Phillies had twenty years earlier, but the punter and holder who was in his third year with the Eagles, bobbled the ball. By the time Hutton got hold of the ball, he was tackled, and the game was over. After posting 10-game winning seasons in 1995 and 1996, hopes were high for 1997. After losing this Monday night game and dropping to 1–2, the Eagles rebounded and improved to 4–4 with a 13–12 win over the Cowboys, but the Eagles won only two of their last eight games and finished 6–9–1. Despite dropping the ball, Hutton was back with the Eagles in 1998, and so was Boniol. The Eagles won only three games, their fewest ever in a 16-game season. The Eagles dropped both matchups with the Cowboys. Ray Rhodes lost his job as Eagles coach and was replaced by Andy Reid. Not only was Rhodes gone, but so was Boniol and Hutton. In Reid's first year, the Eagles beat the Cowboys at the Vet, 13–10, for his first win as Doug Pederson threw a 28-yard touchdown pass to Charles Johnson with 1:07 left in the game.

24 An onside kick.

For only the third time, the Eagles opened up their season against the Cowboys in Texas in 2000. With the temperature at 109 degrees, a good day to be at the beach or indoors with the air conditioning going full blast, the Eagles were opening their second season under Andy Reid, who had some tricks up his sleeve. The Astroturf playing surface made it even hotter. Trainer Rick Burkholder had the players drink pickle juice to prevent dehydration. They drank it in two-ounce shots.

Eagles kicker David Akers began the game with an onside kick which they quickly recovered. Four minutes and one second into the first quarter, Donovan McNabb threw a 1-yard touchdown pass to Jeff Thomason, and the Eagles were on their way. They upped their lead to 24–6 at the half and won it, 41–14.

Duce Staley rushed for 201 yards, four short of the then-club record which Steve Van Buren set in 1949 when he rushed for 205 yards against the Pittsburgh Steelers at Shibe Park. LeSean McCoy broke Van Buren's record when he gained 217 yards in a snowstorm against the Detroit Lions in 2013 at the Linc.

Three years later, with Bill Parcells now coaching Dallas, Reid decided to try an onside kick again to start the game, but Parcells, who had been around the block once or twice was wise to the move. Randal Williams grabbed the kickoff and returned it 37-yards in three seconds for the Cowboys, the fastest touchdown to start an NFL game. The Cowboys went on to beat the Eagles, 23–21.

25 DeMarco Murray.

Very rarely has anyone left the Cowboys for the Eagles or the other way around. Looking to replace LeSean McCoy, who Chip Kelly traded to Buffalo for linebacker Kiko Alonso, the Eagles enticed Murray to leave Dallas, where he led the league in rushing in 2014 with 1,845 yards. McCoy was the Eagles' all-time leading rusher with 6,792 yards, and in 2013, McCoy set the club record for most yards rushing in a season with 1,607 yards. He was the only player in Eagles history to rush for 1,000 or more yards four times in six seasons. McCoy missed four games with the Bills in 2015 but still picked up 895 yards and was back over the 1,000 mark in 2016 when he had 1,267 yards. Murray rushed for 702 yards in 2015, his lone season in Philadelphia before he was traded to Tennessee, where he picked up 1,287 yards for the Titans in 2016.

Many thought that Murray would be the ninth Eagles runner to rush for 1,000 or more yards in a season. He had only one game where he rushed for over 100 yards. Murray only scored six rushing touchdowns.

3

THIRD QUARTER
ALL-PRO LEVEL

ALL-PRO LEVEL

(Answers begin on page 83)

The Eagles have a 19–21 postseason record. They won their first NFL championship in 1948 and followed up by winning their second a year later. The Eagles went back to the NFL Championship Game in 1960 and won their third title. The Super Bowl began six seasons later, and the Eagles have made only two trips to the big game, coming up short both times—against the Oakland Raiders in January 1981 and New England Patriots in February 2005. How well do you know your Eagles postseason history?

1 Against what team did the Eagles play in their first play-off game in 1947?

2 What were the weather conditions when they played in their second NFL championship game in 1948?

3 What NFL record did the Eagles set in the 1949 NFL Championship Game?

4 What game in 1959 that the Eagles won was a preview of what the 1960 season would become?

5 When the Eagles wrapped up the Eastern Conference in 1960, they set a new club record for most consecutive games won with how many?

6 Who scored the winning touchdown in the 1960 NFL Championship Game?

7 Four players from the Eagles' 1960 NFL championship team had previously played for an NFL champion. Who were they?

8 How many players from the 1960 Eagles later became head coaches, assistant coaches, general managers, or personnel directors in the NFL?

9 Who was the first team that the Eagles beat in the regular season that went on to win the Super Bowl?

10 In which season did the Eagles become one of four Philadelphia teams to play for a championship?

11 Where did the Eagles play in their first Super Bowl?

12 Randall Cunningham set the Eagles club record in a postseason game with the most yards passing with 407 against what team?

13 Against what team did the Eagles set their club record against for the most points scored in a postseason game with 58?

14 How many years did it take Andy Reid to coach in the NFC Championship Game?

15 When the Eagles were down to their last play in regulation and facing a 4th-and-26, trailing Green Bay, 17–14, in the 2003 divisional playoff game at Lincoln Financial Field, who did Donovan McNabb complete the pass to and for how many yards?

16 Who did the Eagles beat in the NFC Championship Game in the 2004 season to advance to the Super Bowl?

17 Where did the Eagles play in their second Super Bowl?

18 What three seasons did the Eagles finish in first place after finishing last the previous season?

19 How many Eagles coaches have won their first postseason game?

20 Three quarterbacks for the Eagles hold the team record for the most touchdown passes thrown in a postseason game with three. Who were they?

ALL-PRO LEVEL ANSWERS

1 Pittsburgh Steelers.

The Eagles qualified for the postseason for the first time in 1947. Up through 1966, the only postseason game was the Eastern Conference champion opposing the Western Conference champion for the NFL championship. If there was a tie for first place at the end of the season, as was the case in 1947 with Eagles and Steelers in the Eastern Conference, a playoff game was staged to see who would go on to play the Western Conference champion. Pittsburgh had ended its regular season a week earlier than the Eagles when they beat the Boston Yanks, 17–7, to finish with a 8–4 record. After losing to Green Bay ten straight times, the Eagles beat them the following week, 28–14, at Shibe Park to finish 8–4. Pittsburgh hosted the game at Forbes Field, but the Eagles came away with a 21–0 victory. The first-ever Eagles postseason touchdown was scored by Steve Van Buren, who caught a 15-yard pass from Tommy Thompson in the first quarter. Thompson threw his second touchdown pass in the game in the second quarter, this one for 15 yards to Jack Ferrante. Bosh Pritchard set the postseason club record for the longest return when he bought back a punt 79 yards for a touchdown in the third quarter increasing the Eagles lead to the final score of 21–0.

The win over the Steelers put the Eagles into the NFL Championship Game against the Cardinals in Chicago. During the regular season, the Cardinals beat the Eagles at Shibe Park, 45–21. The NFL had two teams in the Windy City, and the Bears were always the most popular team. They played at Wrigley Field, home of the Cubs, and the Cardinals played their games in Comiskey Park in Chicago. Eventually one team had to move, and it was the Cardinals who packed up and left for St. Louis in 1960.

The Eagles were greeted by bad weather which seemed to be the rule rather than the exception for the NFL championship games in 1947, 1948, and 1949.

The field was frozen, and Steve Van Buren was held to only 26 yards on 18 carries. Tommy Thompson completed 27 of 44 passing attempts for 297 yards. The Cardinals led all the way and scored three touchdowns on long runs. Charlie Trippi score on a 44-yard run, and Elmer Angsman scored on two 70-yard runs. Trippi also scored on a 75-yard punt return.

For the second straight year, Chicago was home to the NFL champion. A year earlier, the Bears had beaten the New York Giants for the championship.

2 A total of 7.4 inches of snow fell that day in Philadelphia.

When Steve Van Buren woke up and saw the snow, he went back to sleep thinking the game would be postponed. He got a phone call to get to Shibe Park which he had to do using public transportation. The tarpaulin was not removed until thirty minutes before game time. Once again, the Eagles were meeting the Chicago Cardinals in the Championship Game.

They had met during the regular season with Chicago winning at Comiskey Park, 21–14.

When the 1948 NFL Championship Game began, the field was covered by snow as soon as the tarpaulin was pulled up. On the Eagles' first play, Tommy Thompson threw a 65-yard touchdown pass to Jack Ferrante. One problem; the play was called back because a player was offside. It was Ferrante.

Late in the third quarter, Elmer Angsman, who burned the Eagles a year earlier in the NFL Championship Game with two 70-yard touchdown runs, fumbled, and Bucko Kilroy recovered on the 17-yard line late in the third quarter which

Steve Van Buren scores the only touchdown of the 1948 NFL Championship Game in the fourth quarter. *AP Photo.*

set up the game's only score in the fourth quarter. Steve Van Buren, who rushed for 98 yards, scored the only touchdown on a 5-yard run in the Eagles' 7–0 victory over the Cardinals to win their first NFL championship.

3 The Eagles became the only team to win two straight NFL championships by shutting out their opponent in both games.

The Eagles won their final eight games in 1949 which was a club record for most consecutive games won to end the season. The Eagles had won their first three games in 1949 before losing to the Chicago Bears, 38–21, at Wrigley Field. The Eagles scored 364 points and gave up only 134 points. This was the only season where the Eagles led the league in most points scored and fewest points given up.

After blanking the Cardinals a year earlier, the Eagles whitewashed the Los Angeles Rams, 14–0, in Los Angeles for their second straight NFL crown. During the regular season season, the Eagles came away with a 38–14 win over the Rams at Shibe Park. The Eagles spent three days getting to Los Angeles by train.

For the third year in a row, the game was played in terrible weather. In 1947, it was cold and the field was frozen in Chicago.

A year later, the Eagles played in the snow at Shibe Park. With everyone looking for a big payday at the Los Angeles Coliseum which seated about 100,000, it rained. Only 22,245 tickets were purchased for the game.

Despite rushing for 196 yards, Van Buren didn't score a touchdown. The Eagles took a 7–0 lead in the second quarter when Tommy Thompson hit Pete Pihos with a 31-yard touchdown pass, and in the third quarter, Leo Skladany, who the Eagles picked up late in the season, blocked a Bob Waterfield punt on the 2-yard line, picked up the ball, and took it into the end zone. The Rams never got past the Eagles 26-yard line. Los Angeles had only seven first downs. The Eagles had 342 net yards while the Rams picked up only 119.

4 They rallied from 24–0 deficit against the Chicago Cardinals.

The Eagles had to come from behind in five of their 10 regular season wins a year later.

Buck Shaw had finished 2–9–1 in 1958, his first year coaching the Eagles. Shaw had told the team that he would have three teams in 1959; one coming, one going, and one playing until he found thirty-five players that wanted to play. Half the team from 1958 wasn't back in 1959. The Eagles started out 2–2 in 1959 including a big 49–21 win over the Giants. The following week, they went to Minnesota to play the Chicago Cardinals, who moved two of their home games from the Windy City to Minnesota. The Eagles fell behind, 17–0, at the half and 24–0 early in the third quarter before they rallied for a 28–24 win. Billy Ray Barnes started the comeback when he scored on a 1-yard rush, and Norm Van Brocklin threw a 29-yard touchdown pass to Tommy McDonald. Barnes scored again on a 2-yard run as the Eagles got to within three points at the end of the third quarter.

With 3:12 to go in the fourth quarter, Van Brocklin threw a 22-yard touchdown pass to McDonald for the winning score. This tied the club record for biggest comeback.

The Eagles went on to finish 7–5, their first winning season in five years. They tied the Browns for second place as the

Giants went on to to win the Eastern Conference for the second year in a row and the third time in four years.

5 The Eagles set the club record for the most consecutive wins with nine in a row.

After losing the season opener to the Browns, 41–24, at Franklin Field, the Eagles took charge with nine straight wins and wrapped up the Eastern Conference in their first appearance against the Cardinals in St. Louis, 20–6. The Eagles lost their next game in the snow at Pittsburgh, 27–21. Several regulars sat out the second half. The Eagles were trailing, 27–0, in the fourth quarter before closing to within six. The Eagles won their final game of the season over Washington, 38–28, in the last game played at Griffith Stadium. In five of those nine wins, the Eagles had to come from behind to win the game in the fourth quarter.

Meanwhile, the Eagles didn't know who they would play in the championship game. When the Eagles clinched the East, Baltimore, Green Bay, and San Francisco were tied for first out West with 6–4 records. Baltimore was trying to win the NFL championship for the third straight season. The Colts, who were 6–2 at one time, went on to do what the 1950 Eagles did while trying to win a third straight NFL championship, dropping four straight games to finish 6–6.

The following week, the Packers moved into sole possession of first place and won the Western Conference in their final game of the season. This put Green Bay into the NFL Championship Game for the first time since 1944 when they beat the New York Giants, 14–7, at the Polo Grounds.

The Eagles also won nine straight games in 2003 and 2017.

6 Ted Dean.

Drafted in the fourth round in 1960, Dean, who graduated from Radnor High School right outside Philadelphia, scored the winning touchdown in the 1960 NFL Championship Game over Green Bay. True to form, in a season when they had to come from behind in five of their ten regular season wins, the championship game was no different.

Christmas had fallen on a Sunday, and the game was played the next day and started at noon because they had to allow for overtime because Franklin Field had no lights. The Packers were favored to win the game. The big news before the game was that Chuck Bednarik was going to play both ways.

Unlike the World Series where home games were shown on local television, the game was blacked out in Philadelphia, and fans either headed far enough north to watch the game on a New York television station in a hotel or headed south to watch the game on a Baltimore station.

On their first two possessions, the Eagles gave up the ball on their 14- and 22-yard lines, and all the Packers got was three points. Green Bay made it 6–0 in the second quarter before Norm Van Brocklin threw a 35-yard touchdown pass to Tommy McDonald for the thirteenth time that season, and Bobby Walston added a 15-yard field goal. The Eagles fell behind in the fourth quarter, 13–10, and began their comeback for the sixth time that season. It started when Dean bought back the kickoff 57 yards.

"Assistant coach Charlie Gauer spotted something in the films about the Green Bay defense on their return team," said Pete Retzlaff. "He felt there were a couple of key blocks that had to be made. Charlie felt there was a wide avenue there the way they covered and had their safetymen back there that left a gapping hole that we took advantage of that. That was the type of coaching that we had, people that were dedicated to spending hours looking at films, trying to pick up little things like that that would help you win a ball game and when you came up with something like that and it was for seven points, it was worth all the hours."

Dean eventually scored on a 5-yard run, and it was his only rushing touchdown of the year. There was 5:21 left in the

Ted Dean (35) heads for the goal line to score the winning touchdown in the fourth quarter of the 1960 NFL Championship Game against Green Bay. *AP Photo.*

game, and the Packers started to come back. They reached the Eagles 22-yard line, and Bart Starr threw a pass to Jim Taylor, who got down to the 8-yard line but was stopped by Bednarik. "I saw the clock winding down," said Bednarik, "and when it hit zero, I told him, 'You can get up now. This game is over.' I was jumping up and down like a cheerleader."

Taylor had 105 yards rushing, more than the entire Eagles team. He went on to have a Hall of Fame career, in fact, nine Packers from this team made the Pro Football Hall of Fame.

7 Chuck Bednarik, Norm Van Brocklin, Stan Campbell, and Jerry Reichow.

Bednarik was a rookie in 1949 when the Eagles won their second straight NFL championship and was the only player who saw action on both the 1949 and 1960 championship teams.

Van Brocklin was with Rams in 1951 and threw a game-winning 73-yard touchdown pass to Tom Fears in the fourth quarter as Los Angeles defeated the Cleveland Browns, 24–17, at the Los Angeles Coliseum. With 7:25 to play in the game, Fears caught the ball at the 50 and was long gone.

Campbell was with the Detroit Lions in 1952 when they traveled to Cleveland and beat the Browns, 17–7. Campbell was in the service and missed the 1953 season when the Lions again beat the Browns for the title, 17–16, at Briggs Stadium. Campbell helped the Lions win another NFL championship in 1957 and once again, Detroit defeated Cleveland, 59–14.

Reichow was backup quarterback for the 1957 Lions and saw action late in the Championship Game, throwing a 16-yard touchdown pass to Howard Cassady for the game's final points.

8 13.

Jerry Reichow held numerous front office jobs with the Minnesota Vikings, Pete Retzlaff became the Eagles general manager for four years beginning in 1969, and Bobby Walston was personnel director with the Chicago Bears.

Norm Van Brocklin (Minnesota and Atlanta), Marion Campbell (Atlanta), and Ed Khayat were head coaches. Campbell (1983–85) and Khayat (1971–72) were head coaches of the Eagles who also served as assistant coaches with the team. Campbell came to Philadelphia after he was let go by the Falcons in 1977 and became Dick Vermeil's defensive coordinator, and Jerry Williams hired Khayat in 1971. Billy Ray Barnes, Maxie Baughan, Jimmy Carr, Bob Pellegrini, Jess Richardson, and Chuck Weber became assistant coaches. Carr and Richardson were assistants with the Eagles.

When Dick Vermeil coached the Eagles for seven years, he hired Chuck Bednarik as an associate coach. Sonny Jurgensen and Tom Brookshier stayed close to the NFL as broadcasters on radio and television.

Two of Buck Shaw's assistant coaches later became head coaches; Nick Skorich, who succeeded Shaw for three years later coached the Browns, and Jerry Williams coached the Eagles for a little over two years.

9 Pittsburgh.

The first Super Bowl winner the Eagles beat was the Steelers in 1979, 17–14. It was Pittsburgh's first trip to Veterans Stadium and only their second visit to Philadelphia since the merger in 1970. The game was tied, 7–7, at halftime before the Eagles went ahead for good in the third quarter on Tony Franklin's 48-yard field goal, and then Wilbert Montgomery ran in a touchdown from the one. This was the fifth straight time that the Eagles beat Pittsburgh at home. The Steelers went on to beat the Los Angeles Rams, 31–19, in Super Bowl XIV.

The following season, the Eagles defeated Super Bowl champion Oakland at the Vet, 10–7. Wilbert Montgomery scored on a 3-yard run with three minutes left.

This was the third meeting between the two teams, and the Raiders had won the first two. Two months later, the two teams met in Super Bowl XV, but Oakland led all the way and won the game, 27–10.

Before the Super Bowl began after the 1966 season, you had to go back to 1955 for the last time the Eagles beat the NFL champion in the regular season when they defeated Cleveland, 33–17, at Connie Mack Stadium.

10 1980.

When the Eagles beat Dallas in the 1980 NFC Championship Game behind Wilbert Montgomery's 194 rushing yards, they completed a sweep of all four Philadelphia professional teams reaching the finals. No other city could boast of four teams playing for a championship in the same season.

In the spring, the Sixers lost the NBA Finals to the Los Angeles Lakers, and the Flyers dropped the Stanley Cup Finals against the New York Islanders. The Phillies won the first championship in team history when they beat the Kansas City Royals in the World Series.

After beating the Minnesota Vikings, 31–16, in the divisional playoff game at the Vet, everyone had to wait to see who the Eagles would play, either Dallas or Atlanta. If the Falcons beat the Cowboys, the NFC Championship Game would be in Atlanta. The Cowboys rallied in the fourth quarter to beat

Atlanta, and Philadelphia was ready for Dallas and they went on to beat the Cowboys, 20–7.

11 New Orleans.

The Eagles had visited New Orleans and beaten the Saints in the Superdome, 34–21, in November. It was the Eagles third trip to New Orleans in three years, and the Eagles had won all the games.

When the Super Bowl began with the National Football League champion meeting the American Football League champion, it was decided to play in a big stadium in warm weather or indoors. This was the fifth time that the Super Bowl was played in New Orleans in the first fifteen years, but just the second time at the Superdome. The first three games were played at Tulane Stadium, home of the Sugar Bowl. The Eagles were favored to win the game and had beaten the Raiders during the regular season, 10–7.

Up to that point, seven times out of eight that a team that went to the Super Bowl for the first time to play a team that had already been there lost. Oakland lost the first Super Bowl they played in, 33–14 to Green Bay, but came back and beat Minnesota nine years later, 32–14. The Eagles made it eight of nine. The Birds never led as the Raiders won the game, 27–10. The Raiders led, 14–0, after the first quarter and 24–3 after three quarters. Jim Plunkett threw three touchdown passes. To make the defeat harder to take was the Eagles lost to the first wild-card team to win the Super Bowl. The Raiders had to play four postseason games to the Eagles' three.

12 Chicago in the "Fog Bowl" in 1988.

The Eagles had won the NFC East for the first time in eight years when they beat the Cowboys in the final game of

Randall Cunningham battles the elements in the "Fog Bowl" playoff game at Chicago in 1988. *AP Photo/Rob Kozloff.*

the year and the Jets beat the Giants. Both teams finished 10–6, but the Eagles won on the tiebreaker and received a bye in the first round of the playoffs, which was the good news. The bad news was they had to go to Chicago where they had never beaten the Bears on the road in eleven tries. Much was made of the fact that maybe the Eagles would have to sneak into Chicago, but Buddy Ryan made sure everyone knew the Eagles had arrived. After everyone got off the plane at the airport and got on the buses to go to the hotel, they headed to Soldier Field with lights flashing and horns honking and circled the stadium.

The Eagles had played in a lot of bad weather during their postseason history, but never on a day like this. It was sunny and cold and then came the fog, which rolled in late in the second quarter and hung around for the second half. Visibility was awful for everyone; players, fans, broadcasters, media, and those watching on TV. The Eagles trailed, 17–9, at the half. Each team could only manage a field goal in the second half. Although Cunningham passed for 407 yards, all the Eagles points came on four Luis Zendejas field goals.

13 Detroit Lions in 1995.

The Eagles made it back to the postseason for the first time in three years when they met the Lions in a wild-card game at the Vet. Detroit, like Philadelphia, had yet to win the Super Bowl, and the Lions hadn't even been there yet. They hadn't won an NFL title in thirty-eight years compared to the Eagles with thirty-five. Both are still waiting to win another one.

Both teams finished 10–6, but the Eagles got home-field advantage for having a better conference record, 9–3 to 7–5. The Eagles came away with an easy 58–37 victory, setting the record for the most points scored in a wild-card game. The game was tied, 7–7, when the Eagles scored 31 straight second-quarter points to set a club record in a postseason game for most points scored in a quarter and made it 44 straight in the third quarter for a 51–7 lead. Rodney Peete led the way, completing 17 of 25 passes for 270 yards and three touchdowns.

The Eagles set a club playoff record for the most net yards gained in a game with 452 and the most interceptions with six.

14 Three years.

In Andy Reid's first year, the Eagles finished 5–11 but a year later, reversed that record to 11–5 and knocked off Tampa Bay at the Vet in the wild-card round, 21–3. Next up for the Eagles were the Giants, who beat the Eagles for the third time that year, 20–10, and made it all the way to the Super Bowl before falling to the Baltimore Ravens, 34–7.

The Eagles were 11–5 in 2001, and that record was good enough for them to win the NFC East for the first time since 1988. The Eagles started off postseason play beating Tampa Bay again at the Vet, 31–9. Then the Eagles traveled to Chicago to meet the Bears in the Windy City. This time the fog stayed away and the Eagles came away with a 33–19 win. Donovan McNabb threw two touchdown passes, scored on a 5-yard run, and David Akers chipped in with four field goals. This put the Eagles into the NFC Championship Game and a trip to St. Louis to play the Rams, who had won the Super Bowl two years earlier under Dick Vermeil. The Rams hung on for a 29–24 win.

15 Freddie Mitchell for 28 yards.

The Packers and Eagles hadn't met in the postseason since 1960 when they met in the divisional round. The Eagles were trailing, 17–14, in the fourth quarter with 2:21 left when they started at their own 20-yard line. Donovan McNabb was sacked by Bhawoh Jue for a 16-yard loss on second down, and an incomplete pass set up 4th-and-26 with 1:12 left. Down to what looked like their last play, McNabb hit Freddie Mitchell with a 28-yard completion to set up a 37-yard field goal by David Akers with five seconds to go. The Eagles won the overtime coin toss, but were forced to punt. Brett Favre, who threw two touchdown passes, was then intercepted by Brian Dawkins, who returned it 35 yards to the Packers 34-yard line. Six plays later, Akers hit the game-winner from 31 yards out with 4:48 gone in overtime.

The next time Green Bay came back to Philadelphia for a playoff game was in 2010. The Packers had snapped their nine-game losing streak in Philadelphia in the opening game that year as they won, 27–10. Proving it was no fluke, the teams met again in a wild-card playoff game at Lincoln Financial Field with Green Bay winning, 21–16, as Aaron Rodgers threw three touchdown passes. To make the loss hurt even more, the Packers went on and won their fourth Super Bowl and thirteenth NFL championship by defeating Pittsburgh, 31–25, in Super Bowl XLV.

16 Atlanta Falcons.

The Eagles made it back to the NFC Championship Game for the fourth straight year and, for the third straight time, the game was in Philadelphia and the second at Lincoln Financial Field. Looking to get over the hump after losses to Tampa Bay two years earlier at the Vet and to Carolina a year earlier, this time the Eagles won it, 27–10, to reach the Super Bowl for the second time.

The Eagles led all the way. Dorsey Levens scored on a 4-yard run in the first quarter to open the scoring. The Eagles made it 14–3 in the second quarter as Donovan McNabb, who was 17-for-26 for 180 yards, threw a 3-yard touchdown pass to Chad Lewis. Atlanta closed to within four before the half ended when Warrick Dunn scored on a 10-yard run. David Akers added two field goals in the third quarter from 31 and 34 yards out. In the fourth quarter, the Eagles wrapped up the game as McNabb threw a 2-yard touchdown pass to Chad Lewis. The defense stood out, holding the Falcons to 202 yards in a game played in a wind chill between zero and five below, much like the Eagles win over Dallas twenty-four years earlier.

17 Jacksonville, Florida.

This was the third city in the Sunshine State to host the Super Bowl following Miami and Tampa.

New England was on a roll in the early part of the twenty-first century. The Patriots had won two of the last three Super Bowls by three points over the St. Louis Rams, 20–17, and the Carolina Panthers, 32–29. Adam Vinateri kicked the game-winning field goal as time expired from 48 yards out against the Rams in 2002 and two years later connected from 41 yards out with four seconds to go over the Panthers.

The Eagles came close to beating the Patriots, but also lost by three points, 24–21.

The Eagles took a 7–0 lead in the second quarter when Donovan McNabb threw a 6-yard touchdown pass to L. J. Smith but New England matched that when Tom Brady threw a 4-yard touchdown pass to David Givens. The Patriots went ahead in the third quarter when Mike Vrabel caught a 2-yard touchdown pass from Brady, but the Eagles answered that when Brian Westbrook caught a pass from McNabb and took it into the end zone on a 1st-and-goal from the 10-yard line. New England made it 24–14 as Corey Dillon ran it in from the 2-yard line, and Adam Vinatieri kicked a 22-yard field goal in the fourth quarter.

The Eagles came back when McNabb hit Greg Lewis with a 30-yard touchdown pass with only 1:48 left in the game. The Eagles attempted an onside kick but New England recovered. After running three plays forcing the Eagles to use their last three timeouts, New England punted the ball away. There were 46 seconds left, and the Eagles were starting from their own 4-yard line. Three plays later, McNabb threw his third interception, the fourth Philadelphia turnover in the game.

New England matched the Cowboys' feat of winning three Super Bowls in four years.

18 In 2006, 2013, and 2017.

After setting the club record for the most wins in a season with 13 in 2004 and going to the Super Bowl, the Eagles dropped to last and went only 6–10 in 2005. Terrell Owens was deactivated by the team and missed nine games, and Donovan McNabb had missed the final seven games when he had to undergo surgery for a sports hernia. There were other injuries during the season as well. The Eagles came back strong in 2006 and finished 10–6, winning their final five games and winning the NFC East for the fifth time in six years.

In 2012, the Eagles finished in last place with a 4–12 record. Chip Kelly replaced Andy Reid, and the Eagles went 10–6 and finished in first place. They started out 3–5 but came on strong and won seven of their last eight games to finish 10–6 and won the NFC East championship. Kelly became the first Eagles coach to finish in first place in his first year at the helm. The Eagles improved by six victories and this was the second time they accomplished this.

The first time was in 2000 when they went 11–5 in Andy Reid's second year. He had inherited a team that was 3–13 in 1998 and he went 5–11 in 1999 before reversing the record in 2000 as the Eagles went on to make it to the postseason for the first time in four years.

The Eagles also began their most successful decade in team history and the best five-year period was from 2000 to 2004 when the Eagles won 59 games and lost 21. Andy Reid set the club record for the most consecutive years making the playoffs with five and the most consecutive times finishing in first place with four straight years beginning in 2001. The Eagles won three straight conference titles from 1947 to 1949 but after that never finished in first two straight years until 2002. They were Eastern champs in 1960, 1980, and 1988 before winning four straight from 2001 to 2004. In 2017, Doug Pederson, after finishing with a 7–9 record in his first season in 2016, saw his team go 13–3 and have home field advantage all the way though the NFC playoffs.

19 Five: Greasy Neale, Buck Shaw, Rich Kotite, Ray Rhodes, and Andy Reid all won the first postseason game they coached for Philadelphia. When Neale's Eagles met the Steelers in their first postseason game in 1947, it was a playoff to see who would play the Chicago Cardinals for the NFL championship. The Eagles and Steelers had finished tied for first in the Eastern

Conference, and the Eagles came away with a 21–0 win at Forbes Field.

Shaw only coached the Eagles for three years. In Shaw's final year in 1960, the Eagles won the NFL championship with a 17–13 win over Green Bay at Franklin Field. Shaw retired after the game.

The next coach to win his first postseason game was Kotite in 1992. Philadelphia went down to New Orleans and knocked off the Saints, 36–20, in a wild-card game. They next had to face the Cowboys in Texas, but it was Dallas who came away with the win, 34–10. To make matters worse, after beating the 49ers for the NFC title, the Cowboys went to the Super Bowl and beat Buffalo, 52–17.

What made this loss tough for the Eagles was in the fourth game of the year, they had easily defeated the Cowboys at Veterans Stadium, 31–7, in a Monday night game.

In Rhodes's first year at the helm in 1995, the Eagles defeated Detroit at the Vet, 58–37, in the highest scoring postseason game in Eagles history. The following weekend they fell to Dallas, 30–11.

After a losing season in 1999, Reid got the Eagles back to postseason play in his second season, and they started with a win over Tampa Bay at the Vet, 21–3, in a wild-card game. Trying to avoid losing to the Giants three times in one season, the Eagles dropped a 20–10 contest in a divisional playoff game.

20 Ron Jaworski, Rodney Peete, and Donovan McNabb.

Jaworski was the first to throw three touchdown passes for the Eagles in a postseason game. The Eagles were back in the wild-card game in 1979 at Veterans Stadium after

Ron Jaworski was the first Eagles quarterback to throw three touchdown passes in a postseason game. *AP Photo/Clem Murray.*

losing to the Falcons in Atlanta a year earlier, 14–13, and were facing the Chicago Bears and their defensive coordinator, Buddy Ryan. Jaworski hit Harold Carmichael for touchdowns twice, from 17 and 29 yards. With the score tied, 17–17, in the fourth quarter, Jaworski and Billy Campfield hooked up on a 63-yard touchdown pass as the Eagles beat the Bears, 27–17.

Peete was the next to throw three touchdown passes in a postseason game as the Eagles routed the Lions, 58–37, at Veterans Stadium in 1995. Peete threw his three touchdown passes to Fred Barnett (22 yards), Rob Carpenter (43 yards), and Ricky Watters (45 yards).

The Eagles got back to the Super Bowl in the 2004 season and lost to New England, 24–21, in Jacksonville. In that game, McNabb threw touchdown passes to L. J. Smith for six yards, Brian Westbrook for 10, and Greg Lewis for 30.

McNabb threw three touchdown passes a second time four years later in the NFC Championship Game against the Cardinals in Arizona. The Eagles had trailed, 24–6, when McNabb bought the Eagles back. He threw two touchdown passes to Brent Celek from six and 31 yards out and gave the Eagles the lead when he threw a 62-yard touchdown pass to DeSean Jackson in the fourth quarter. It wasn't enough as the Cardinals came back and won the game, 32–25.

4

FOURTH QUARTER
HALL OF FAME LEVEL

FOURTH QUARTER

HALL OF FAME LEVEL

(Answers begin on page 113)

We begin the final quarter by testing your knowledge of Eagles quarterbacks through the years.

1 Four Heisman Trophy-winning quarterbacks played for the Eagles. Who were they?

2 Although he could see out of only one eye, Tommy Thompson took the Eagles to the NFL Championship Game three times and won twice. In 1948, Thompson led the league in touchdown passes. How many did he throw?

3 Who was the first Eagles quarterback to throw for over 400 yards in a game?

4 How many Eagles quarterbacks also served as the club's punter?

5 Five times the Eagles made a deal for a quarterback with the Rams. Who did they trade for?

6 What quarterback set the club record for throwing the most touchdown passes to the same receiver in a 12-game season?

7 Carson Wentz set a new club record in 2017 with 33 touchdown passes. Whose record did he break?

8 When Joe Kuharich took over as the coach on February 27, 1964, it took him less than three months to trade away two future Hall of Fame players, flanker Tommy McDonald and quarterback Sonny Jurgensen. After Jurgensen was traded to Washington along with cornerback Jimmy Carr for quarterback Norm Snead and defensive back Claude Crabb, quarterback was a real problem for the Eagles for the next 13 years until Dick Vermeil came in 1976 and a year later picked up Ron Jaworski. From 1964 to 1976, how many different quarterbacks started for the Eagles?

9 Who threw the longest touchdown pass in Eagles history?

10 Who were the only Eagles quarterbacks to throw three touchdown passes of 70 yards or more in a season?

11 What Eagles quarterback threw the most touchdown passes to the same receiver in a career?

12 Who holds the Eagles record for the most consecutive games throwing a touchdown pass?

13 Who was the first Eagles quarterback to throw for 300 yards or more in three straight games?

14 MATCH THE QUARTERBACK WITH THE PLAYER THAT HE THREW HIS FIRST TOUCH-DOWN PASS TO WITH THE EAGLES:

1.	Randall Cunningham	a.	Rocky Ryan
2.	Ron Jaworski	b.	Larry Cabrelli
3.	Sonny Jurgensen	c.	Chad Lewis
4.	Donovan McNabb	d.	Earnest Jackson
5.	Norm Snead	e.	Clarence Peaks
6.	Tommy Thompson	f.	Tom Sullivan
7.	Norm Van Brocklin	g.	Timmy Brown

15 Who was the last Eagles quarterback to call his own plays?

16 Only two quarterbacks in Eagles history had a perfect quarterback rating in a game, 158.3. Who were they?

17 Who set the Eagles record for the most rushing touchdowns by a quarterback in a season?

18 Which two quarterbacks hold the Eagles record for the most fourth-quarter comebacks in a season with five?

19 When the Eagles defeated the Cardinals at the Vet, 38–14, in 2002, Donovan McNabb threw four touchdown passes. An hour after the game, the Eagles made an announcement about McNabb's condition. What was it?

20 When Steve Van Buren retired, how many NFL rushing league records did he hold?

21 Which Eagles receiver led the league in pass receptions three years in a row?

22 What Eagle caught the most touchdown passes of 70 yards or longer in a career?

23 Who were the first trio of Eagles to gain 100 yards or more receiving in the same game?

24 Who are the only three Eagles players to lead the league in scoring?

25 The Eagles began retiring numbers after 1951 and retired their most recent in 2013. Who are the nine players that have had their number retired and what are their numbers?

26 Who holds the club record for the most different ways scoring a touchdown in a season?

27 Who holds the club record for most different ways scoring a touchdown in a career?

28 The most points the Eagles have ever scored against the Green Bay Packers was 47 in 2004 when they beat them, 47–17. Donovan McNabb, Terrell Owens, and Andy Reid each set a new club record that day. What records did they each break in that game?

29 The team record for the most touchdowns scored in a game is four set by six players. Who was the only player to do it twice?

30 Five players have had five seasons where they caught 50 or more passes in a season five times. Who was the first?
   a. Keith Byars
   b. Harold Carmichael
   c. Jeremy Maclin
   d. Pete Retzlaff
   e. Brian Westbrook

31 What Eagle was the first player to lead the league in interceptions in consecutive years?

32 Chicago Cardinals quarterback Jim Hardy set an NFL record for throwing the most interceptions in a game with eight against the Eagles in 1950. What Eagles player tied an NFL record in that game for the most interceptions with four?

33 Who was the only Eagles player to score two touchdowns on interceptions in a game and tied the NFL record for the most touchdowns scored on interception returns in a season?

34 Who set the club record for the most opponent fumble recoveries in a season?

35 Who was the Eagles' last straight-ahead kicker?

36 Who holds the club record for kicking the most field goals of 50 yards or longer in a season?

37 Since joining the National Football League in 1933, the Eagles have been in the Eastern Conference/Division of the NFL/NFC. How many different teams have been in the Eastern Conference/Division with the Eagles?

38 The Eagles won all their home games during a season four times. In what years did they accomplish this feat?

39 The Eagles' club record for the most shutouts in a season is four, which they have done twice. What years were they? And who was the only team that the Eagles shut out twice in a season?

40 What was the most times the Eagles scored 40 or more points in a game and in what season?

HALL OF FAME LEVEL ANSWERS

1 Davey O'Brien, John Huarte, Ty Detmer, and Sam Bradford.

O'Brien of Texas Christian University was selected by the Eagles in the first round of the 1939 NFL draft. He was the first Eagles draft pick to win the Heisman Trophy in 1938, just the fourth year that the award was given out. O'Brien played two seasons with the Eagles.

Huarte of Notre Dame won the award in 1964. He was drafted by the Eagles and the New York Jets of the American Football League in 1965 and signed with the Jets even though they had also drafted Joe Namath ahead of him. Huarte did very little in the AFL or NFL. He played seven games for the Eagles in 1968 but made only one start.

The next to win the Heisman Trophy was Detmer from Brigham Young University in 1990. After spending four years with the Packers, Detmer spent two years with the Eagles in 1996 and 1997.

The most recent Eagles quarterback who had won the Heisman Trophy was Bradford of Oklahoma in 2008. Bradford was drafted by the St. Louis Rams, but he was traded to the Eagles before the 2015 season along with a 2015 fifth-round draft choice (traded to Miami) for Nick Foles, a fourth-round draft choice in 2015, and a second round draft choice in 2016. Bradford stayed one season and was traded to the Vikings eight days before the start of the 2016 season for a first-round draft pick in 2017 and a fourth round pick in 2018.

2 25 in 1948.

The Eagles played anywhere from nine to 12 games a year from 1933 to 1946. Beginning in 1947, the NFL played a 12-game schedule through 1960. Only once did someone throw more touchdown passes in a season before Thompson threw 25 in 1948. Sid Luckman of the Chicago Bears tossed 28 in 1943. Pete Pihos caught 11 from Thompson, a personal high and a club record at the time. Thompson also threw six touchdown passes to Jack Ferrante, two each to Neill Armstrong, Russ Craft, and Bosh Pritchard, and one each to Joe Muha and Ernie Steele. His longest was to Craft for 70 yards while Thompson set the club record at time for the most touchdown passes in a game with four against the Boston Yanks and Detroit at Shibe Park.

When Thompson retired after the 1950 season, he had thrown 90 touchdown passes, a club record at the time which was broken in 1970 by Norm Snead, who threw 111. Ron Jaworski threw 175 touchdown passes to surpass Snead's record, and Donovan McNabb now owns the record with 216. Thompson was the first Eagles quarterback to pass 10,000 yards when he finished with 10,240. Thompson was selected All-Pro in 1948 and 1949, beating out Sammy Baugh, Sid Luckman, and Bob Waterfield.

He was also the first of three players, but the only quarterback in club history, to throw a touchdown pass and catch a touchdown pass in the same game in 1941 as the Eagles fell to the Brooklyn Dodgers at Shibe Park, 24–13. Foster Watkins threw an 8-yard touchdown pass to Thompson and Tommy threw a 50-yard touchdown pass to Larry Cabrelli. In fact, this was Thompson's first touchdown that he scored with the Eagles and it came before he threw his first touchdown pass with the club.

Harold Carmichael was the second Eagle to catch a touchdown pass and throw one in the same game as the Eagles lost to the Baltimore Colts, 22–21, at the Vet in 1983. He threw a 45-yard touchdown pass to Mike Quick and caught an eight-yard touchdown pass from Ron Jaworski.

The third player to accomplish the feat was Keith Byars in a 31–0 win over Green Bay at Veterans Stadium in 1990. He threw eight yards to Anthony Toney and caught a 12-yard touchdown from Randall Cunningham.

3 Bobby Thomason in 1953.

Thomason passed for 437 yards as the Eagles defeated the Giants, 30–7, at Connie Mack Stadium. Thomason completed 22 of 44 passes for 437 yards and threw four touchdown passes, two each to Bobby Walston and Pete Pihos. Thomason's 437 yards passing in a game was the fourth highest in NFL history at the time. His team record held up until 1989 when Randall Cunningham broke it when he threw for 447 yards against Washington at RFK Stadium. Thomason's 437 yards is still the fourth highest in Eagles history.

Thomason is one of only seven Eagles quarterbacks to throw for over 400 yards in a game. In his last year with the Eagles in 1957, wins were few and far between. In a 38–21 win over the Cardinals at Comiskey Park, Thomason became the first Eagles quarterback to score two touchdowns and throw two touchdown passes in the same game. This was only the second win of four as the Eagles lost eight games, their third losing season in a row. He threw touchdown passes to Bill Stribling for 58 yards and to Bobby Walston for 21 yards. The Eagles were leading, 17–14, when the fourth quarter began and Thomason scored twice on 1-yard runs.

As much as Adrian Burk and Thomason took turns playing at quarterback, Thomason made it to the Pro Bowl after the 1953 and 1955 seasons, and Burk made it after the 1954 and 1955 seasons. When they both made the Pro Bowl in 1955, it was the first time that two quarterbacks from the same team in the Eastern Conference were selected in the same year.

4 Six.

For their first forty or so years, the Eagles had a position player that not only did all the kicking but also did all the punting. In those days, squads were approximately 35 players per team and some players had to do extra things like punt, place kick, or hold for the kicker.

Davey O'Brien was the first Eagles quarterback that handled some of the punting duties in 1939 and 1940. Next up was Roy Zimmerman for four years beginning in 1943. Adrian Burk was the full-time punter for six years beginning in 1951. He still holds the club record for the most punts in a career with 393. When the Eagles traded for Norm Van Brocklin, they not only got a quarterback, but their new punter as well. When the Dutchman retired after the Eagles won the championship in 1960, they signed King Hill as the backup quarterback to Sonny Jurgensen for 1961, and Hill handled the punting for his first three years and split the punting duties with Sam Baker for the next three. The last was Randall Cunningham who did an excellent job as a punter when he was called upon from time to time.

Cunningham also set the club record in 1989 for the longest punt when he got off a 91 yarder at Giants Stadium with the wind at his back. That was the third longest punt in NFL history. On the next play, Mike Golic forced a fumble and the Eagles scored three plays later on Keith Byars's 2-yard run, giving the Eagles a 24–17 win. Cunningham only punted 12 times with the Eagles but this one was the most important. His second longest was 80 yards in 1994.

5 Bobby Thomason, Norm Van Brocklin, Roman Gabriel, Ron Jaworski, and Sam Bradford.

The Eagles made five trades for quarterbacks with the Rams, four when they were in Los Angeles and one when they were based in St. Louis. The first quarterback that the Eagles received from the Rams was Thomason who had spent the 1949 season with Los Angeles. Getting any playing time there was near impossible. The Rams had two future Hall of Famers, Bob Waterfield and Van Brocklin. Thomason went to Green Bay, but after the 1951 season, he was returned to the Rams. From there, it was on to Philadelphia where he and Adrian Burk, who had come from Baltimore after the 1950 season, took turns starting. There was a lot of controversy on who should be the starter. Some fans wanted Burk and others preferred Thomason. Coach Jim Trimble usually went with the guy with the hot hand. Thomason faced his former team three times and three times the Rams came away victorious behind starting quarterback Van Brocklin.

The second quarterback that came over from the Rams was Van Brocklin, who wasn't happy in Los Angeles after Sid

Gilliam became the coach in 1955. Van Brocklin had led the league in passing twice before Eagles general manager Vince McNally swung a deal in 1958, sending offensive tackle Buck Lansford, defensive back Jimmy Harris, and their number one draft pick in 1959 to the Rams. It has to rank as one of the greatest deals in Eagles history. Only once did Dutch get to face his old team, and it resulted in a 23–20 Eagles win at

Norm Van Brocklin poses with coach Buck Shaw a few days before he led the Eagles to victory in the 1960 NFL Championship Game against the Green Bay Packers. *AP Photo.*

Franklin Field in 1959 as another former Ram, Paige Cothern, kicked a tie-breaking 14-yard field goal with 16 seconds left in the game.

Gabriel came to Philadelphia in 1973 and the Eagles paid a heavy price for him, including Harold Jackson, a wide receiver who led the league in receiving yards in 1969 and 1972, fullback Tony Baker, the Eagles' number one draft picks in 1974 and 1975, and a 1975 third-round draft pick. It wasn't until 1975 that Gabriel got a chance to beat his former team but he probably wished the Rams weren't on the schedule. Los Angeles wiped out the Eagles, 42–3, in a Monday night game. By halftime, the Vet was half empty.

Vermeil had been an assistant coach with the Rams in 1973 when Ron Jaworski joined the team. After spending two years with UCLA and winning the Rose Bowl in 1976 over No. 1 Ohio State, 23–10, Vermeil came to Philadelphia. After spending one year on the sideline, Vermeil swung into action and acquired Jaworski for tight end Charle Young. This deal, along with the one for Van Brocklin, certainly ranks as one of the top deals in Eagles history. Jaws faced the Rams five times, and he won two and lost three. His first win came in 1983 when he threw a 29-yard touchdown pass to Tony Woodruff with 20 seconds to go at the Vet to give the Eagles a 13–9 victory, and three years later got his second win over his former team, 34–20. Jaworski was 17-for-27 and threw for 213 yards including three touchdown passes. He connected with John Spagnola for 15 yards, Mike Quick for 55 yards, and Junior Tautalatasi for 16 yards. It was also the first win for new coach Buddy Ryan.

The Rams had moved out of Los Angeles to Anaheim in 1980, but still remained the Los Angeles Rams. In 1995, the Rams packed up and moved to St. Louis. They have since moved back to Los Angeles. Before the Rams started their final season in St. Louis, the Eagles traded Nick Foles to the Rams and picked up Bradford, who stayed one year. After the Eagles drafted Carson Wentz, the Eagles traded Bradford to the Vikings. Bradford never got to face his former team as a member of the Eagles.

6 Norm Van Brocklin to Tommy McDonald in 1960.

Van Brocklin and McDonald hooked up 12 times in the regular season and added a thirteenth in the NFL Championship Game against Green Bay. Although they only played three seasons together for a total of 36 regular season games, the Dutchman found McDonald 29 times, which was also a club record at the time. The two also teamed up one more time in the Pro Bowl after the win over Green Bay for a fourteenth.

Sonny Jurgensen tied Van Brocklin's record the following year when he threw 12 touchdown passes to McDonald. The record was tied twenty-two years later by the duo of Ron Jaworski and Mike Quick.

In 2004, Donovan McNabb broke that record when he threw 14 touchdown passes to Terrell Owens. Only ten times in club history has a quarterback teamed up with the same receiver on 10 or more touchdown passes in a season. Tommy Thompson threw 11 touchdown passes to Pete Pihos in 1948 and Randall Cunningham threw 11 to Quick in 1987.

Four times, the same quarterback teamed up on 10 touchdown passes in a season with the same receiver. Sonny Jurgensen found Tommy McDonald 10 times in 1962, and five years later, Norm Snead threw 10 touchdown passes to Ben

Hawkins. Jaworski threw 10 to Harold Carmichael in 1979 and 10 to Quick in 1985.

7 Sonny Jurgensen threw 32 touchdown passes in 1961.

With the retired Norm Van Brocklin now coaching the expansion Minnesota Vikings, the Eagles turned to Sonny Jurgensen to keep the offense rolling in 1961. He did more than that, tying the NFL record set by Johnny Unitas of Baltimore for the most touchdown passes in a season with 32 to seven different receivers. His favorite target was Tommy McDonald, who caught 12 touchdown passes, and Pete Retzlaff, who caught eight. Dick Lucas caught five, Billy Ray Barnes had three, Bobby Walston with two, and Tim Brown and Ted Dean each caught one. Jurgensen threw touchdown passes in 13 of the 14 games, but in the biggest win of the year when they beat the Cowboys at the Cotton Bowl, 43–7, Jurgensen failed to throw a touchdown pass. He more than made up for that when Dallas came to Franklin Field. The Eagles had dropped two straight on the road to the Giants and Browns by a combined 38 points, and when the offense was introduced before the game, Jurgensen was booed and fans were yelling for King Hill. In a 35–13 victory, Jurgensen threw five touchdown passes— three to McDonald, and one each to Dean and Retzlaff.

Injuries set Jurgensen back the following season when he threw only 22 touchdown passes. He threw 65 touchdown passes as a starter in his last three years after playing behind Bobby Thomason and Van Brocklin for four years.

The next time Jurgensen threw five touchdown passes in a game at Franklin Field was when he faced the Eagles for the first time after being traded to the Washington Redskins.

Everyone knew that Joe Kuharich made a bad trade by swapping Jurgensen for Norm Snead and this game convinced everyone that the deal would come back and haunt the Eagles, which it did for the next 11 years. Wentz set the record of 33 in just 13 games in 2017 before suffering a season-ending knee injury against the Rams in Los Angeles.

8 13.

Norm Snead made most of the starts from 1964 to 1967. King Hill and Jack Concannon were the backups. Snead had his best season in 1967 with 29 touchdown passes, but in 1968 he broke his leg in the first preseason game against the Lions at Franklin Field and missed the rest of the preseason and the first three games of the regular season. Hill became the starter until Snead came back, and eventually Hill was traded to the Vikings. The Eagles picked up John Huarte, who never did much in the AFL and much less in the NFL after winning the Heisman Trophy in 1964, but he contributed little. Snead was back as the full-time starter in 1969 and 1970, but owner Leonard Tose was not happy with him. General manager Pete Retzlaff traded Snead to the Minnesota Vikings for tackle Steve Smith and three draft picks. Greg Barton was acquired from Detroit but he never took a snap with the team. Instead of coming east, he headed north to play in the Canadian Football League. Pete Liske started in 1971 and 1972 but he wasn't the answer. Mike McCormack became the Eagles coach in 1973, and he followed what his former boss, George Allen, said with the Redskins that the future is now. He got Roman Gabriel but paid a heavy price. Gabriel had one solid year in 1973. He was benched at the end of the 1974 season and at the end of the 1975 season. Gabriel sat out the first 10 games of the 1976 season with injuries before starting the last four games of the year. The following March, Dick Vermeil swung into action and acquired Ron Jaworski from the Rams.

Starting Records for Eagles Quarterbacks, 1964–76

Norm Snead	1964–70	28–50–3
King Hill	1964–68	5–12–1
Jack Concannon	1964–66	3–0
John Huarte	1968	0–1
George Mira	1969	0–1
Rick Arrington	1970–73	1–3–1
Pete Liske	1971–72	7–9–1
John Reaves	1972–75	0–7
Roman Gabriel	1973–76	12–25–1
Mike Boryla	1974–76	8–10
Total	1964–76	63–113–6

During this period, the Eagles had three other quarterbacks: Benjy Dial in 1967, Jim Ward in 1971–72, and John Walton in 1976 that were backups but didn't start. Walton backed up Ron Jaworski for the next three years.

9 Ron Jaworski to Mike Quick, 99 yards.

Only 13 times in NFL history has a quarterback connected on a 99-yard touchdown pass and only once was it done in overtime when Jaworski connected with Quick to give the Eagles a 23–17 win over the Falcons at Veterans Stadium in 1985.

The Eagles had jumped out to a 17–0 lead but the Falcons came back with 17 straight points in the fourth quarter to send the game into overtime. Atlanta won the toss but was forced to punt. Rick Donnelly got off to a 62 yarder that went out of bounds on the Eagles 1-yard line. On second down, Jaworski threw a pass to Quick which he caught at the 20-yard line between cornerback Bobby Butler and safety Scott Case. After Quick caught the ball, he easily made it into the end zone with 2:49 gone in overtime.

Broadcaster Merrill Reese described the play:

"Here it is, second down and ten for the Eagles. Jaworski on second down. Retreats. He is looking. He fires the football. Complete to Quick. He is going to go. 25, 30, 35, 40, midfield, 45, 40, 35, 30. Mike Quick touchdown. The Eagles win. The Eagles win.

"Forget the field goal. Jaworski to Quick, 99 yards and an all-time Eagles record, Jaworski to Quick and the game is over."

Six different Eagles quarterbacks have thrown touchdown passes of 90 yards or longer. Randall Cunningham, Jaworski, and Donovan McNabb have each done it twice," but Jaworski is the only one to throw his 90-plus yard touchdown passes to same receiver, Quick. The first time was in 1984 at the Vet when Jaworski hit Quick on a 90-yard pass in a losing cause against the Cardinals.

10 Adrian Burk and Jim McMahon.

Burk led the NFL in touchdown passes with 23 in 1954 and three of those were 70 yards or longer. Burk threw an 80-yard touchdown pass to Jerry Williams against the Cardinals in Chicago and later teamed up with an 84-yard touchdown pass to Williams at Connie Mack Stadium against Washington. Both times, the Eagles came away with a win. His third was in Detroit to Bobby Walston for 75 yards as the game ended in a 13–13 tie.

McMahon took over in the first game of the 1991 season at Green Bay after a knee injury sidelined Randall Cunningham for the year. In the fourth quarter, McMahon threw a 75-yard touchdown pass to Fred Barnett. His second went to Keith Jackson for 73 yards at the Vet against the Giants, and he teamed up again with Fred Barnett on a 70-yard touchdown pass a week later at Cleveland as the Eagles won all three games.

11 Ron Jaworski to Harold Carmichael with 47.

Harold Carmichael made the Pro Bowl four times. Here he catches a pass in his record-breaking 106th consecutive game in 1979 against the Cleveland Browns. *AP Photo/Gene Puskar.*

Jaworski and Carmichael spent seven years together with the Eagles. Carmichael spent his first six years with the Eagles with five different quarterbacks under Jerry Williams, Ed Khayat, and Mike McCormack. Dick Vermeil was hired in 1976 and made a trade with the Rams the following year that bought Jaworski to Philadelphia.

Carmichael still holds the club record for the most touchdowns scored with 79. He made the Pro Bowl four times. Jaworski spent two years backing up Dan Marino in Miami and in 1989 spent his final season as a reserve with Kansas City.

Jaworski set the club record for the most consecutive games started by a quarterback with 116. His streak ended with three games to go in the 1984 season against the Cowboys at home. A week earlier, he broke his leg in St. Louis. Jaws was back playing the full schedule in 1985, but in 1986, in the tenth game of the season, he broke his finger on his throwing hand. It not only ended his season, but his career with the Eagles. He was not offered a contract for 1987.

Jaworski also threw 33 touchdown passes to Mike Quick, second most in Eagles history followed by Sonny Jurgensen with Tommy McDonald when they hooked up 30 times until both were traded away after the 1963 season.

12 Randall Cunningham, 18 straight games from 1987 to 1988.

Cunningham's streak started in the first game of the 1987 season. He played in 12 of the 16 scheduled games starting with the first two. The NFL strike followed, and Week Three was cancelled and the following three weeks, replacement players were used, although some of the other teams had a few of their regular players, including Danny White and Tony Dorsett of

Dallas, cross the picket line and played in those games. Buddy Ryan wanted his players to stay together; either everyone come in or everyone stay out. All of the Eagles players elected to stay out. When the regular players returned for the final 10 games, winning six and losing four, Cunningham ran his streak to 12 straight games and followed up by throwing touchdown passes in the first six games of the 1988 season. His streak was stopped by the Browns in Cleveland as the Eagles lost, 19–3.

Cunningham had always been a threat to run the ball when he quarterbacked the Eagles. His biggest years as a runner were his first six years with the Eagles before a knee injury in the first quarter of the first game of the 1991 season put him out for the year. Between 1985 and 1990, he rushed for 23 touchdowns but only nine more in his last four years with the Eagles. Injuries cut his 1993 season short, and two years later in his final season in Philadelphia, he lost his starting job to Rodney Peete.

Before Cunningham's arrival, the last Eagles quarterback who was a threat to run with the ball was Jack Concannon, who had been the first quarterback in team history to rush for over 100 yards in a game. He was selected by the Eagles in the second round of the 1964 draft. His first start of the 1966 season came against the Steelers in Week Twelve at Franklin Field, where he picked up 129 yards rushing on 15 attempts. The Eagles were leading Pittsburgh by four points in the fourth quarter when Concannon scored on a 1-yard run to put the Eagles ahead, 27–16. They held on for a 27–23 win. It was the Eagles' seventh win of the year against only five losses. Before the 1967 season, he was traded to the Chicago Bears for Mike Ditka.

13 Donovan McNabb was the first Eagle to throw for 300 yards or more in three straight games in 2005. His streak started in the home opener in the second game of the season as the Eagles defeated San Francisco, 42–3. McNabb completed 23 of 29 passes including five for touchdowns and he threw for 342 yards. Facing another team from the West Coast at home the following week, the Eagles defeated Oakland as McNabb completed 30 of 52 passes for 365 yards and two more touchdown passes. The Eagles next went to Kansas City, and McNabb passed for 369 yards as he completed 33 of 48 passes and threw three more touchdown passes. With the Eagles off to a 3–1 start, it looked like another trip back to the playoffs but McNabb's streak ended in Dallas as the Cowboys came away with 33–10 win. The Eagles went 3–9 the rest of the season.

Michael Vick was next to throw for 300 or more yards in a game three straight times. His streak started in the final game of the 2011 season at the Linc as he threw for 335 yards in a 34–10 win over Washington. Vick continued his streak in 2012 throwing for 317 yards on Opening Day in Cleveland and followed up with 371 yards against the Ravens at the Linc as the Eagles started 2–0, but after that, the Eagles season went in reverse as they won just two of their last fourteen games.

Nick Foles started off the 2014 season throwing for 300 or more yards in the first three games as the Birds got off to a 3–0 start. He passed for 322 yards in the opener as the Eagles beat Jacksonville at the Linc, 34–17. The following week, he threw for 331 yards at Indianapolis in a 30–27 win over the Colts, and back home a week later, he passed for 411 yards against Washington as the Eagles defeated the Redskins, 37–34.

Foles got hurt in the eighth game of the season and Mark Sanchez took over and became the fourth Eagles quarterback to pass for 300 or more yards in a game three straight weeks. His streak began when he passed for 332 yards as the Eagles beat Carolina, 45–21, at the Linc. The following week at Lambeau Field, Sanchez threw for 346 yards but it was all Green Bay as they beat the Eagles, 53–20. Back home a week later, Sanchez threw for 307 yards as the Eagles knocked off Tennessee, 43–24.

The most recent to throw for 300 or more yards in three straight games was Sam Bradford who did it in the final three games of the 2015 season. The Eagles dropped the first two games, 40–17 to the Cardinals and 38–24 to the Redskins, both at home. Bradford threw for 361 yards against Arizona and passed for 380 yards against Washington. Chip Kelly was fired after the loss to Washington, and in the only game under interim coach Pat Shurmur, Bradford threw for 320 yards at MetLife Stadium as the Eagles beat the Giants, 35–30. Bradford never got a chance to become the first quarterback in Eagles history to make it four straight games as he was traded right before the 2016 season to Minnesota.

14 Here are the answers to Match the Quarterback with the Player That He Threw His First Touchdown Pass to with the Eagles:

1.	Randall Cunningham	d.	Earnest Jackson
2.	Ron Jaworski	f.	Tom Sullivan
3.	Sonny Jurgensen	a.	Rocky Ryan
4.	Donovan McNabb	c.	Chad Lewis

5.	Norm Snead	g.	Timmy Brown
6.	Tommy Thompson	b.	Larry Cabrelli
7.	Norm Van Brocklin	e.	Clarence Peaks

Thompson started his Eagles career in 1941 under new coach Greasy Neale. He threw his first touchdown pass to Cabrelli in a losing cause as the Eagles were beaten by the Brooklyn Dodgers, 24–13, at Shibe Park.

Jurgensen was drafted by the Eagles in 1957 and made his first start against the Cleveland Browns in the fourth game of the season. The Eagles had dropped their first three games and Hugh Devore decided to give Jurgensen a start. The Eagles went on to beat Cleveland, 17–7, at Connie Mack Stadium. Jurgensen's first touchdown pass was to Rocky Ryan for 46 yards and he later scored a touchdown on a quarterback sneak.

Brocklin joined the Eagles in 1958 after spending his first nine years with the Rams. The Dutchman threw his first touchdown pass to Clarence Peaks in his second game with the Eagles as they jumped out to a 7–0 lead over the Giants at Franklin Field. The Eagles went onto to beat New York, 27–24.

Snead came to the Eagles in a trade that sent Jurgensen packing to Washington.

Snead made his Eagles debut in the opening game of the 1964 season at Franklin Field, a 38–7 win over the Giants, throwing his first touchdown pass to Timmy Brown for six yards.

Jaworski made his debut with the Eagles against Tampa Bay at the Vet in 1977. His first touchdown pass went to Tom Sullivan for seven yards and it gave the Eagles a 7–0 lead, and they went on to to beat the Buccaneers, 13–3.

Playing in his third game of the year and his second as a starter in his rookie season of 1985, Cunningham threw his first touchdown pass to Earnest Jackson for 17 yards as the Eagles beat Washington, 19–6, at RFK Stadium.

McNabb threw his first touchdown pass from six yards out to Chad Lewis in his second start, a 44–17 loss to the Indianapolis Colts in 1999 at Veterans Stadium. He had started his rookie season under new coach Andy Reid as a backup to Doug Pederson, but made six starts during the second half of the season.

15 Roman Gabriel.

Coaches calling plays for the quarterbacks is not something new. It actually started when Paul Brown, who coached the Cleveland Browns from 1946 to 1962, called plays for the quarterback. The way to get those plays to the huddle those years was using alternate messenger guards. During the 1950s, most quarterbacks called their own plays. When Tom Landry became the first coach of the expansion Dallas Cowboys in 1960, he called the plays. Every Eagles coach allowed the quarterback to call his own plays until Dick Vermeil took over in 1976. With Gabriel sidelined until the last four games of the season, Mike Boryla had his plays called for him. Gabriel had played in Los Angeles and called the plays when Vermeil was an assistant coach there.

When it was announced that Gabriel was healthy enough to come back and take over for the last four games of the season, Vermeil was asked who would call the plays and he never hesitated, saying Gabe would call his own plays. With Ron Jaworski on board starting in 1977, Vermeil went back to calling the plays, and all quarterbacks with the Eagles since have had their plays called for them.

16 Donovan McNabb and Nick Foles.

McNabb was the first Eagles quarterback to have a prefect rating of 158.3 when he led the Eagles to a 56–21 win over the Detroit Lions at the Linc in 2007. McNabb completed 21 of 26 passes including four for touchdowns and passed for 381 yards. He threw three of his four touchdown passes to Kevin Curtis for 68, 12, and 43 yards as the Eagles jumped out to a 42–21 lead at the half. The 42 points was a club record at the time for the most scored in the first half. This was the third time that the Eagles scored 56 points in game, eight short of the record that they set in 1934 over the Cincinnati Reds at Temple Stadium when they put 64 on the scoreboard.

The 56 points was a club record for the most points scored in a regular season game against the Lions, but in 1995, the Eagles scored 58 points against Detroit in a wild-card game at the Vet.

Before he was traded to Washington after the 2009 season, McNabb set the club records for most passing attempts (4,746), most completions (2,801), most yards (32,873), and he threw the most touchdown passes (216).

Foles achieved his perfect quarterback rating when the Eagles traveled to Oakland and beat the Raiders, 49–20, in 2013. Nick tied both the club and NFL records for the most touchdown passes thrown in a game with seven. Foles was 22-of-28 and passed for 406 yards although he sat out a good deal of the game once the Eagles were up, 49–13, late in the third quarter. After his seventh touchdown pass, Foles directed the Eagles on two more drives with no success, and he was taken out of the game rather than risk an injury trying to throw his eighth touchdown of the game.

In 2013, he set the club record for the highest quarterback rating in a season with 119.2, which is the third best in NFL history. Foles set the club record at the time for highest completion percentage in a season with 64 percent. His touchdown/interception ratio of 27/2 was best in NFL history, and he is the only quarterback in league history to throw for 20 or more touchdowns in a season and have two or fewer interceptions. Foles was traded to the St. Louis Rams after the 2014 season.

17 Michael Vick.

Vick took over as the starting quarterback in 2010 after backing up Donovan McNabb the previous year. The most rushing touchdowns by a quarterback had been set in 1977 by Ron Jaworski with five in his debut season with the Eagles. Randall Cunningham broke Jaworski's record eleven years later with six and McNabb tied Randall's record twice, in 2000 and 2002. In 2010, Vick set the new record when he ran it into the end zone nine times.

Bobby Thomason had been the first Eagles quarterback to rush for two touchdowns and throw two touchdown passes in the same game in 1957 at Chicago against the Cardinals. The Eagles won the game, 38–21. Jaworski matched that in 1977 at the Vet in a 28–7 win over New Orleans.

Vick was able to run for two touchdowns and he threw four touchdown passes in the same game in 2010 as he led the Eagles to a 59–28 win over Washington on the road. It was the most points the Eagles scored in an away game and it was the second highest overall.

18 Norm Van Brocklin and Randall Cunningham with five.

Van Brocklin brought the Eagles back in the fourth quarter five times in 1960 including three in a row when the Eagles ran their record to 8–1. Van Brocklin's first comeback was at Franklin Field when Tommy McDonald caught an 11-yard touchdown pass against the St. Louis Cardinals with 6:27 to go, giving the Eagles a 31–27 victory. The second was two weeks later when the Eagles were visiting the Browns, who had beaten the Eagles on Opening Day, 41–24, at Franklin Field. The Eagles fought an uphill battle but had closed the gap to one point before Bobby Walston kicked a 38-yard field with 10 seconds to play. In November, the Eagles were struggling against Washington, and it was late in the fourth quarter that the Eagles took the lead for good when the Dutchman threw a 28-yard touchdown pass to Walston, putting the Eagles ahead for good, 16–13, and they won the game, 19–13. Next up were back-to-back games against the Giants beginning in Yankee Stadium. The Eagles were behind at halftime, 10–0, but rallied and tied the game, 10–10, and won it when Jimmy Carr recovered a fumble and returned it 38 yards for a touchdown. The following week back at Franklin Field, the Eagles fell even further behind. They trailed, 17–0, at the end of the first quarter and were behind, 23–17, when the fourth quarter began, but Van Brocklin threw touchdown passes to Ted Dean for 49 yards and Billy Ray Barnes for 8 yards.

Cunningham's five comebacks took place in 1989. First, he threw a 4-yard touchdown pass to Keith Jackson with 52 seconds to go as the Eagles rallied for a 42–37 win over Washington at RFK Stadium. With 2:18 to go against the Giants at the Vet, Anthony Toney scored on a 2-yard run. Comeback number three for Cunningham came when the Eagles beat the Broncos in Denver, 28–24. Keith Byars scored the winning touchdown with 5:25 left in the game. The fourth comeback came when the Eagles beat the Vikings at the Vet, and Cunningham threw a 3-yard touchdown pass to Cris Carter with 2:32 to go to win the game. For the second time that season, the Eagles had to come from behind to beat the Giants, this time at Giants Stadium, as Byars scored on a 2-yard run with 4:10 gone in the fourth quarter.

19 Donovan McNabb was sacked early in the game against the Cardinals. He mentioned to the trainers that he thought his ankle was sprained and they kept taping him up. He completed 20 of 25 passes for 255 yards including touchdown passes to James Thrash, Dorsey Levens, Todd Pinkston, and Duce Staley. No x-rays were taken during the game but after the game, x-rays showed his ankle was broken, and he was finished for the regular season. The Eagles won the game, 38–14. There were six games left and the Eagles were 7–3. A. J. Feeley won four of five starts, and Koy Detmer won his lone start as the Eagles ended the season with a 12–4 record and finished in first place in the NFC East for the second straight year. They also matched their season high in wins as they last won 12 games in 1980. McNabb returned in time for the playoffs, and the Eagles had home-field advantage all the way through. After losing to the Rams a year earlier in the NFC Championship Game on the road, their mission was to get home-field advantage and they did. First up, the Eagles beat Atlanta, 20–6. Bobby Taylor intercepted a Michael Vick pass and returned it 39 yards for a touchdown as the Eagles took a 7–0 lead and never looked back. The Eagles were up, 13–3, in the fourth quarter when McNabb threw a 35-yard touchdown pass to James Thrash. It looked like the Eagles might make it back to the Super Bowl, but they lost to Tampa Bay, 27–10, in the last game at the Vet in the NFC Championship Game.

20 Nine.

Steve Van Buren set the record for leading the league in rushing the most times with four in 1945, 1947, 1948, and 1949, and he set the record for the most consecutive seasons leading the league with three straight from 1947 to 1949. Both records were broken by Jim Brown of Cleveland.

Van Buren also set the record by for leading the league in rushing attempts four times from 1947 to 1950. That record was also broken by Brown. Van Buren set a record for the most consecutive seasons, with the most rushing attempts during those four seasons. Walter Payton later tied Van Buren's record with the Bears beginning in 1976.

He set the record for the most times leading the league in rushing touchdowns with four (1945, 1947–49). Brown surpassed that record in 1965 in his last year with the Browns. Van Buren set the record for the most consecutive seasons leading league in rushing touchdowns with three (1947–49). His record was tied by Brown (1957–59), Abner Haynes of the Dallas Texans (1960–62), and Leroy Kelly (1966–68) with the Cleveland Browns. Cookie Gilchrist of the Buffalo Bills (1962–64) and Denver Broncos (1965) did it four years in a row.

Van Buren set the record for the most touchdowns scored in a season with 18 in 1945 in a 10-game season breaking the record set by Don Hutson of Green Bay who had 17 in 1942. Brown tied Van Buren's record with 18 in 1958 and Jim Taylor of Green Bay broke it in 1962 when he found the end zone 19 times.

Van Buren set the record for the most yards gained in a season with 1,146 in 1949, and Brown came along and broke it nine years later when he rushed for 1,527 yards.

Van Buren also retired as the number one rusher with 5,860 yards and Brown also broke this record.

21 Pete Pihos from 1953 to 1955.

Pihos played nine seasons with the Eagles beginning in 1947. He was drafted in 1945 by the Eagles, but had been taken into the service before that. In his final three years, he led the league in pass receptions starting in 1953 with 63. The following season, he caught 60 passes, tying Billy Wilson of San Francisco, and in his last year led the league a third straight time when he caught 62 passes. Many were shocked when he called it a career. He made All-Pro seven times on offense, missing in 1951, and made All-Pro as a defensive end in 1952. When the Pro Bowl resumed in 1950, Pihos made it six straight seasons.

Pihos had been an offensive end with the Eagles for his first five years with the team (1947–51) but he was moved to defensive end in 1952 and was replaced by Bud Grant, who had been a defensive end in 1951. Pihos played some offensive end in 1952, catching 12 passes and scoring one touchdown. Grant left the Eagles after the 1952 season and jumped to the Canadian Football League, and Pihos was switched back to offense. Grant had caught 56 passes, two short of the club record of 58 set by Joe Looney in 1940. Grant had 997 yards receiving, a club record at the time, which Pihos broke the following year when he had 1,049 yards. Tommy McDonald broke Pihos's record in 1961 when he caught 64 passes totaling 1,144 yards. Pihos had set the club record for the most touchdown receptions in a season with 11. McDonald broke that record in 1960 when he caught 13, which Mike Quick tied in 1983. Terrell Owens surpassed that mark in 2004 with 14.

22 Mike Quick spent nine years with the Eagles beginning in 1982 and set the club record with five touchdown receptions of 70 yards or more. He teamed up with Ron Jaworski on his first four. In 1983, they combined on an 83-yarder at Dallas and a year later, they combined on a 90-yarder at the Vet against the St. Louis Cardinals. In 1985, Jaworski and Quick hooked up twice; a 82-yard pass at San Francisco, and back at the Vet a week later, Quick caught his 99-yard touchdown pass to beat Atlanta in overtime. His fifth came a year later when Randall Cunningham threw a 75-yard touchdown pass to him against the New York Giants at the Vet.

Injuries cut Quick's career short. He was only able to play in a total of 18 games during his final three years. Before that, he made the Pro Bowl five times. In 1983, Quick set the club record for the most yards receiving in a season with 1,409 and tied Tommy McDonald's record (since broken) for the most touchdown passes caught in a season with 13. He is tied for third in club history with Pete Pihos for the most touchdown passes caught with 61. Quick was the first Eagles receiver to catch 70 or more passes in a season with 73 in 1985. He also set the club record for most times catching 60 or more passes in a season with four.

23 Timmy Brown, Tommy McDonald, and Pete Retzlaff.

The Eagles were playing out the string at the end of the 1960 season when they played their final game of the year against Washington in the last NFL game played in Griffith Stadium. The Eagles had wrapped up the Eastern Conference two weeks earlier when they beat the Cardinals, 20–6, at Busch Stadium.

Norm Van Brocklin played only the first half and Sonny Jurgensen played the second half but Brown, McDonald, and Retzlaff all went over the century mark in receiving yards. McDonald did it in the first half. He caught only two passes on the day from Van Brocklin for 116 yards. The first was for a 52-yard touchdown and the second was another touchdown pass from the Dutchman covering 64 yards. McDonald's last touchdown reception set the club record at the time for the most touchdown passes caught in a season with 13. Jurgensen threw two touchdown passes in the second half. His first was to Brown for 34 yards and the second was to Retzlaff for 57 yards. Brown caught five passes for 128 yards and Retzlaff caught five passes for 110 yards as the Eagles beat Washington, 38–28.

The only other time the Eagles had three players go over 100 yards receiving in the same game came in the 2008 season opener at the Linc when DeSean Jackson had 106 yards on six catches, Greg Lewis caught five passes for 104 yards, and Hank Baskett totalled 102 yards on only two receptions including a 90-yard scoring pass from Donovan McNabb. The Eagles went on to beat the St. Louis Rams that day, 38–3.

24 Steve Van Buren, Bobby Walston, and David Akers.

Van Buren led the league in scoring in 1945 when he scored 18 touchdowns, a club record at the time, and added two extra points. Van Buren scored 15 rushing touchdowns, caught two touchdown passes, and returned a kickoff for a touchdown. He even found time to play some defense, intercepting one pass. Van Buren also rushed for 832 yards, averaging 5.8 yards per carry. He set the club record that season for the most touchdowns rushing in a game with three in the final game of the season in a 35–7 win over the Boston Yanks at Shibe Park. Van Buren was selected to the All-Decades squad for the 1940s.

Walston, who was the first Eagle to be named Rookie of the Year in 1951, was next to lead the league in scoring with 114 points, in 1954. Walton scored 11 touchdowns, kicked 36 extra points, and added four field goals. He set the club record that season for the most points scored in a game with 25 against Washington at Griffith Stadium as the Eagles beat the Redskins, 49–21, as Adrian Burk tied the NFL record for the most touchdowns passes thrown in a game with seven. Walston was selected to the All-Decade team of the 1950s.

Akers was the last Eagle to lead the NFL in scoring in 2010 when he put 143 points on the board. Akers kicked 32 field goals and added 47 points and finished one point ahead of Sebastian Janikowski of Oakland. This was his last year with the Eagles as he finished as their all-time club leader in points with 1,323. Akers led the National Football Conference three times in scoring; 2004 with 122 points and in 2008 and 2009 when he was league runner-up with 144 and 139 points. Akers went on to set the club record for the most game-winning field goals with 10.

25 Steve Van Buren (15), Al Wistert (70), Tom Brookshier (40), Chuck Bednarik (60), Pete Retzlaff (44), Jerome Brown (99), Reggie White (92), Brian Dawkins (20), and Donovan McNabb (5).

The Eagles have retired nine numbers beginning with Van Buren and Wistert. Van Buren was with the Eagles from 1944 to 1951. Injuries slowed him down in his final two years. A knee injury during training camp in 1952 ended his career. He was inducted into the Pro Football Hall of Fame in 1965.

Wistert played with the Eagles from 1943 to 1951. For some reason, his number 70 had been issued again but was taken out of circulation for good after the 1972 season. In nine years with the Eagles, he was voted All-Pro five times.

Brookshier's number 40 was retired after the 1961 season. Nobody knew it at the time but his career ended in the eighth game that season when he broke his leg against the Bears at Franklin Field. Brookshier attempted to return without success in 1962 and called it a career after seven years with the Eagles, later becoming a popular sportscaster.

At the end of the 1962 season, Bednarik retired after 14 seasons with the Eagles and his number 60 was retired right away. Concrete Charlie's next stop was the Hall of Fame, where he was inducted in 1967.

The next number to be retired by the Eagles was number 44 for Retzlaff, who played in Philadelphia from 1956 to 1966. Nicknamed "the Baron," he held most of the team's receiving records upon his retirement.

The Eagles didn't honor another player until the start of the 1992 season when number 99 was retired for Brown, who

Chuck Bednarik had his number 60 retired following his retirement in 1962. *AP Photo*.

had been killed in an automobile accident on a rain-soaked road in Brooksville, Florida, on June 25. Brown had joined the Eagles in 1987. The Eagles retired his number on Opening Day.

White joined the Eagles in 1985 and left as a free agent after the 1992 season. He later played with Green Bay and Carolina. His number 92 was retired by the Eagles on December 5,

2005, and he was inducted into the Pro Football Hall of Fame the following summer.

Dawkins, who wore number 20 and spent 13 years with the Birds beginning in 1996, was the next Eagles player to have his number retired. The Eagles were the second team in Philadelphia to retire number 20 after the Phillies retired Mike Schmidt's number in 1989.

McNabb was the most recent player to have his number retired. He spent 11 years with the Eagles starting in 1999 and held almost all of the Eagles passing records. His number 5 was retired before the Eagles-Chiefs game on September 19, 2013.

Three players that played for the Eagles had their number retired by other teams—Cris Carter, Mike Ditka, and Reggie White. Ditka had played six years with the Chicago Bears before he joined the Eagles in 1967 and left after the 1968 season. The Bears retired his number 89. The Minnesota Vikings retired number 80 for Carter, who spent 12 seasons with the Vikings. The Packers retired number 92 for White, who spent six years in Green Bay. White is the only player in the NFL to have his number retired by two teams.

26 Bosh Pritchard, Timmy Brown, and Brian Mitchell.

In 1948, Pritchard became the first Eagles player to score a touchdown four different ways in a season. He scored his first touchdown when he caught a 34-yard touchdown pass from Tommy Thompson in a 21–14 loss to the Cardinals in Chicago on Opening Day. The following week, Pritchard scored on a 52-yard run against the Rams in Los Angeles as the Eagles, who had led in this game 28–0, ended up tied, 28–28, as Bob Waterfield bought the Rams back. Pritchard scored touchdowns his third and fourth different ways that season in Week Six when the Eagles traveled across the state and defeated the Steelers, 34–7, at Forbes Field. Pritchard scored on a 55-yard punt return and later returned a fumble 18 yards for a touchdown.

Brown scored touchdowns four different ways in the same season in both 1961 and 1962. He scored his first touchdown in the season opener at Franklin Field when he returned the opening kickoff 105 yards as the Eagles beat Cleveland, 27–20. Eight games later, Brown scored on a 16-yard pass reception from King Hill as the Eagles fell to the New York Giants at Yankee Stadium, 38–21. Brown scored touchdowns his third and fourth different way in Week Twelve that season when he returned a punt 66 yards for a touchdown and scored on a 42-yard run as the Eagles defeated Pittsburgh at Forbes Field, 35–24. The following year, Brown once again scored on Opening Day, and once again it was on a return, only this time it was a missed field goal attempt by St. Louis kicker Gerry Perry that Brown took back 99 yards. Later in the game, which the Eagles lost to the Cardinals at Franklin Field, 27–21, he scored on a 1-yard run. The following week, when the Eagles lost to the Giants at Franklin Field, 29–13, Brown caught a 14-yard touchdown pass from Sonny Jurgensen. Later in the season, Brown returned a kickoff 99 yards against Washington at District of Columbia Stadium, helping the Eagles to defeat the Redskins, 37–14.

Mitchell was the third Eagles player to score a touchdown four different ways in a season and he did it despite scoring a total of only five touchdowns in 2000. Mitchell scored his first in an Opening Day win over the Cowboys in Dallas, 41–14, when he scored on a 6-yard run. His next touchdown came in Week

Four on a punt return which he bought back 72 yards in New Orleans as the Eagles beat the Saints, 21–7. His third touchdown that year came a week later when he took a kickoff back 89 yards as the Eagles toppled the Falcons at the Vet, 38–10. Mitchell's fourth different way to score a touchdown that season came a month later at Pittsburgh when he caught a 13-yard pass from Donovan McNabb as the Eagles, playing for the last time at Three Rivers Stadium, won, 26–23, in overtime.

27 Bosh Pritchard and Timmy Brown.

Pritchard was the first Eagle to score a touchdown five different ways. The first was a 97-yard kickoff return in 1942 against Washington at Griffith Stadium in a 30–27 loss to Redskins, who went on to win the NFL championship over an undefeated Chicago Bears team. Pritchard scored touchdowns his second and third different ways in a 49–25 win over the Boston Yanks at Shibe Park in 1946. First, Pritchard scored on a 68-yard run and, later in the game, caught a 35-yard touchdown pass from Tommy Thompson. Two years later, Pritchard scored touchdowns a fourth and fifth different way against the Steelers at Forbes Field. He returned a punt 55 yards for a touchdown and later scored on a fumble recovery from 28 yards out as the Eagles came away with a 34–7 win.

Brown was the other player to score a touchdown for the Eagles five different ways. His first two came in the 11th game of the 1960 season after the Eagles had clinched the Eastern Conference. Used mainly on punt and kickoff returns all season, Brown saw quite a bit of playing time at Pittsburgh in a snow storm. He scored his first touchdown on a pass from Sonny Jurgensen that covered 53 yards and scored on a 7-yard run later in the game. Brown didn't waste any time scoring a touchdown a third different way when he took the opening kickoff on Opening Day in 1961 and ran it back 105 yards for a touchdown. Later that season, he returned a punt 66 yards for a touchdown helping the Eagles beat the Steelers, 35–24, at Forbes Field. Brown scored a touchdown a fifth different way when he scored a 99-yard touchdown on a missed field attempt on Opening Day in Franklin Field against the Cardinals in 1962.

28 Andy Reid had the most wins by Eagles coach, Donovan McNabb had the most yards passing in a game and most consecutive passes completed, and Terrell Owens had the most touchdown passes caught in a season.

Reid was in his sixth season coaching the Eagles when he won his 67th game, 47–14, over the Packers at the Linc in 2004. Reid broke the record set by Hall of Fame coach Greasy Neale, who won 66. Reid coached the Eagles from 1999 to 2012 and won 130 games, lost 93, and had one tie. In his 14 years with the Eagles, he made the playoffs nine times and finished first six times. Reid was fired after the 2012 season but was quickly hired by the Kansas City Chiefs, making it the second time that a former coach of the Eagles took over the Chiefs. The first was Dick Vermeil.

McNabb passed for 464 yards, breaking the record set by Randall Cunningham, who threw for 447 yards at Washington in 1989. McNabb completed his last 10 passes a week earlier against the Giants in the Meadowlands and his first 14 passes against the Packers.

The 24 straight completions set an NFL record (since broken by Ryan Tannehill of the Miami Dolphins) and his 14 straight pass completions is an NFL record for the most to start a game.

Owens caught his 14th and final touchdown pass of the season to set a new club record. Tommy McDonald had set the old record when he caught 13 touchdown passes in 1960 and 1961. Mike Quick tied the record in 1983. Owens caught 77 passes, sixth best in a season at the time in Eagles history and his 1,200 yards receiving was fifth best at the time. Owens was hurt in the 14th game and was done for the regular season. He missed the first two playoff games but played in the Super Bowl and caught nine passes for 122 yards.

29 Wilbert Montgomery scored four touchdowns in a game twice, both times against Washington. Montgomery did it for the first time in the second game of the 1978 season at RFK Stadium when he scored on runs of 34 yards in the first quarter and 10 yards in the third quarter. The Eagles, who had trailed 35–16, closed to within five when Montgomery scored on an 8-yard run and a 5-yard run in the fourth quarter. Washington still held on for the win, 35–30. A year later at the Vet, Montgomery scored four touchdowns in a game for the second time as the Eagles beat the Redskins, 28-17. He scored on an 8-yard run in the first quarter and caught an 11-yard touchdown pass from Ron Jaworski in the second quarter. He scored his final two touchdowns in the third quarter on runs of 5 and 4 yards.

Montgomery later became the first Eagles running back to score a rushing touchdown in the Pro Bowl in 1979 when he scored on a 2-yard run to put the NFC ahead, 6–0, and they won the game, 13–7, when Roger Staubach threw a 19-yard touchdown pass to Tony Hill, his Dallas Cowboys teammate.

Montgomery spent eight years with the Eagles before he was traded to Detroit and was the Eagles' leading ground gainer at the time with 6,538 yards and ranked second in rushing touchdowns with 45. He was the first player in club history to have three 1,000-yard rushing seasons in 1978, 1979, and 1981. Montgomery was also the first to do it back-to-back in 1978 and 1979.

30 d., Pete Retzlaff.

Five players hold the club record with five seasons with 50 or more pass receptions. Retzlaff was the first, beginning in 1958 when he tied Raymond Berry of the Baltimore Colts for the league lead with 56. Retzlaff had 50 receptions in 1961, and then had three straight years with 50-plus receptions with 57 in 1963, 51 in 1964, and 66 in 1965.

Four other Eagles have had 50 or more pass receptions in a season five times: Harold Carmichael was the next in 1973–1974, 1978–1979, and 1981. Keith Byars was the first to do it five straight years beginning in 1988. Brian Westbrook also had five in consecutive years (2004 to 2008) followed by Jeremy Maclin from 2009 to 2012 and 2014.

The first time the Eagles had four players with 50 or more receptions in a season was 2011. Maclin had 63 receptions while Brent Celek was next with 62. DeSean Jackson had 58 and Jason Avant had 52. The following year, three of the players from 2011 were also in the next group of four with 50 passes caught. Maclin once again led the way with 69, Celek had 57, and Avant had 53. LeSean McCoy was the fourth that year with 54 receptions. The third and most recent season where the Eagles had four players all catch 50 or more passes in a year was 2014. Maclin led with 85 receptions followed by Jordan Matthews with 67, Zach Ertz, 58, and Riley Cooper, 55.

Only twice have the Eagles had three players with 60 or more receptions in a season. In 1984, John Spagnola led the team with 64 while Mike Quick caught 61 and Wilbert Montgomery had 60. In 2007, Brian Westbrook led with 90 receptions, setting the club record for the most in a season. Kevin Curtis caught 77 passes and Reggie Brown had 61 receptions.

There have been six seasons in which Eagles had two players with 70 or more receptions. In 1988, rookie Keith Jackson caught 81 passes and Keith Byars 72. It wasn't until 2004 that the Eagles had two players with 70 or more receptions in a season for a second time when Terrell Owens had 77 and Westbrook 73. Three years later, Westbrook caught 90 and Kevin Curtis 77. In 2010, McCoy hauled in 78 passes and Maclin 75. In 2015, Matthews caught 85 passes and Ertz 75. These same two players went over the 70 mark again the following season as Ertz caught 78 passes and Matthews had 73.

31 Bill Bradley was the first player to lead the league in interceptions two straight years. He had 11 in 1971 and nine the following season. His 11 in 1971 is still the club record and his nine in 1972 matched Ed "Bibbles" Bawel in 1955 and Don Burroughs in 1960. Asante Samuel also had nine interceptions in 2009.

Bradley joined the Eagles in 1969 and spent eight years with the team, setting the club record for the most interceptions with 34, since tied by Eric Allen and Brian Dawkins.

Bradley was named an All-Pro from 1971 to 1973 and was selected to the Pro Bowl following those seasons.

The first Eagles player to lead the league in interceptions was quarterback Roy Zimmerman. He picked off 19 passes from 1943 to '46, leading the league with seven in 1945. Zimmerman was not the first full-time quarterback to lead the league in interceptions. Sammy Baugh set an NFL record at the time with Washington when he picked off 11 passes in 1943. Troy Vincent picked off seven passes and tied for the league lead in 1999 and Asante Samuel had nine in 2009, also tied for league lead. A year later, Samuel came within one of leading the league when he had seven, but he still led the NFC.

32 Russ Craft.

The Eagles had lost their season opener in 1950 to Cleveland, 35–10, after winning consecutive NFL championships in 1948 and 1949. This was the first game for the Browns in the National Football League after winning all four All-America Football Conference championships from 1946 to 1949. Looking to get back on the winning track, the Eagles headed to Chicago to play the Cardinals at Comiskey Park. There were thirteen teams in the National Football League that year and each team received one bye week. The Cardinals had their bye in the first week of season. Craft picked off four of Jim Hardy's eight interceptions, tying the NFL record for the most in a game. Joe Sutton had three interceptions and Frank Reagan the other as the Eagles beat the Cardinals, 45–7. The Cardinals also turned the ball over four times on fumbles as the Eagles tied the NFL record for most recoveries in a game with 12.

The following week, when the Eagles beat the Los Angeles Rams at Municipal Stadium, 56–20, Craft set the Eagles record for the longest kickoff return (since broken) when he bought one back 103 yards for a touchdown. It looked like the Eagles might have a good chance to become the first team to win the NFL championship three straight years since the Championship Game was started in 1933. They won five straight but after losing to Pittsburgh at Shibe Park, 9–7, the Eagles ran their record to 6–2 when they traveled to Griffith Stadium and beat Washington, 33–0. No one knew it at the time, but this to be was last win for coach Greasy Neale. The Eagles lost their final four games by a total of 16 points.

Eric Allen holds the Eagles team record for most interceptions returned for a touchdown with five. *AP Photo/Bill Feig.*

33 Eric Allen tied the NFL record for most interceptions returned for a touchdown in a game with two against New Orleans in 1993. Allen picked off Steve Walsh twice and returned them 33 and 25 yards, leading the Eagles to a 37–26 win at the Vet.

That season, Allen also set the Eagles club record and tied the NFL record for the most interceptions returned for a touchdown in a season with four. He collected his first in the third game of the season as the Eagles beat Washington at the Vet, 34–31. Allen returned Cary Conklin's pass for a 29-yard score. After a bye week, the Eagles traveled up the New Jersey Turnpike and knocked off the New York Jets at Giants Stadium, 35–30. Midway through the fourth quarter, the Eagles were trailing the Jets, 30–28, when Allen picked off Boomer Esiason at the Eagles 6-yard line and returned it 94 yards. Allen had led the NFC with eight interceptions in 1989, the most he ever had in a season.

Allen also holds the club record for the most interceptions returned for a touchdown with five. His first was in 1990 when he intercepted Babe Laufenberg in 1990 at the Vet and returned it 35 yards for a touchdown as the Eagles beat the Cowboys, 17–3.

Allen played seven years with the Eagles and tied with Bill Bradley for most interceptions with 34. He made All-Pro in 1989, 1991, and 1993. Allen was selected for the Pro Bowl in 1989 and from 1992 to 1995.

34 Vic Sears was the first Eagles player to recover three opponents fumbles in a game and only the second player in the NFL at the time, but it came in a losing cause. The Eagles fell to the

Green Bay Packers in Milwaukee, 12–10, in 1952. The Eagles played the Packers in Milwaukee only four times, and lost all four. Things were looking good for an Eagles win in the fourth quarter as they were leading, 10–6. Adrian Burk went back to punt for the Eagles, but it was blocked, and John Martinkovic picked up the ball on the 5-yard line and took it into the end zone for the game-winning touchdown. This loss came back to hurt the Eagles at the end of the season. They finished tied for second place with the New York Giants with a 7–5 record, but Cleveland won the conference with an 8–4 record.

Sears was the first Eagles player to play for the team 13 years, a club record that held up until Chuck Bednarik broke it when he played his 14th season in 1962. A standout offensive and defensive lineman, Sears was selected to the NFL All-Decade team of the 1940s. The Eagles had just as tough a time over the years beating the Packers in Green Bay. They lost seven straight there before winning in 1979.

35 Tom Dempsey.

Pete Gogolak was the first-ever soccer-style kicker in the AFL or NFL. He was with the Buffalo Bills in 1964 and 1965 before switching leagues and signing with the New York Giants in 1966. Many thought a soccer-style kicker wouldn't make it in pro football, but before anyone knew it, more and more teams were picking up these type of kickers. Dempsey, who had set the NFL record at the time for kicking the longest field goal from 63 yards with New Orleans in 1970, was signed by the Eagles during the 1971 season. Happy Feller, who was drafted in the fourth round in 1971, lasted just nine games. The Eagles released Feller and picked up Dempsey who stayed through 1974. Beginning in 1975, the Eagles have had nothing but soccer-style kickers.

Prior to the advent of soccer-style kickers, Bobby Walston was the only Eagles placekicker to lead the league in scoring with 114 points in 1954. Walston scored 11 touchdowns to go with his four field goals and 36 extra points.

After Horst Muhlmann replaced Dempsey in 1975, Dick Vermeil had problems finding a reliable kicker. He tried Ova Johansson in 1977 before settling on Nick Mike-Meyer, who stayed for the rest of the season and was the placekicker in 1978. Then in the "Miracle at the Meadowlands" game that season, Mike-Meyer was attempting an extra point but the ball was snapped high and when he tried a pass, got hurt and was done for the year. For the first time in ten years when Sam Baker did it, a punter, Mike Michel, had to do double duty punting and placekicking for the Eagles.

That season, an extra wild-card team was added to the playoffs, and the Eagles met the Falcons in Atlanta. The Eagles were leading, 13–0, before the Falcons came back to take a 14–13 lead. With 13 seconds to go in the game, Michel, who had earlier missed an extra point, attempted a 34-yard field goal but missed. At the end of the season, Michel and Mike-Meyer were gone. Third-round draft pick Tony Franklin was the new kicker, and he was the first the Eagles player that kicked barefooted.

36 Jake Elliott in 2017.

Elliott took over the placekicking duties from Caleb Sturgis in the second game of the season and, in Week 3 against the Giants, kicked a 61-yard field goal—the longest in team history, as time expired, giving the Eagles a 27–24 win at the Linc. The following week, Elliott kicked a 53-yard field goal against the Chargers. Elliott's third field goal of 50 yards or longer came on the road against the Carolina Panthers on October 12 and a week later back at the Linc, he booted a 50 yarder against Washington. Elliott set the club record with his fifth 50-plus yard field goal against the 49ers on October 29.

Cody Parkey (2014) and Sturgis (2016) held the old record with four.

37 Ten:

Atlanta Falcons	1966
Boston/Washington Redskins	1933–Present
Boston Yanks/New York Bulldogs	1944–1949
Brooklyn Dodgers/Tigers	1933–1944
St. Louis/Phoenix/Arizona Cardinals	1960–2001
Cleveland Browns	1950–1969
Dallas Cowboys	1961–Present
New Orleans Saints	1967–1969
New York Giants	1933–Present
Pittsburgh Steelers	1933–1942, 1945–1969

Atlanta joined the National Football League in 1966 as its fifteenth franchise and every team had a bye week that year. The Falcons played each team once before moving to the Western Conference when New Orleans became the sixteenth franchise in 1967 and was placed in the Eastern Conference.

The Falcons second-ever game was against the Eagles at Franklin Field with the Eagles coming out on top, 23–10. Brooklyn folded after the 1944 season and the Bulldogs moved to the National Conference (the NFL had National and American conferences from 1950 to 1952) in 1950, changing their name to the Yanks.

The Eagles played the Cardinals on the road in five different cities. The last meeting for the Eagles on the road against the Chicago Cardinals took place in Minnesota in 1959 before the Vikings joined the NFL two years later.

Games against Cleveland and Pittsburgh on a regular basis became a thing of the past when those teams joined the American Football League teams to make up the American Football Conference in 1970 when the two leagues merged. Up until this time, Cleveland had won four NFL championships and the Steelers none. Since the merger, Cleveland has yet to play in the Super Bowl while Pittsburgh has led the way with six victories.

Playing the Cardinals every year stopped after the 2001 season and the Eagles still play the Cowboys, Giants, and Redskins regularly.

38 In 1945, 1948, 1949, and 1992.

The Eagles joined the NFL in 1933 but it wasn't until they merged with the Pittsburgh Steelers for the 1943 season that they had their first winning season. In 1944, the Eagles went from being good to great, culminating with winning NFL championships in 1948 and 1949. The Eagles' first undefeated season at home came in 1945 when the Eagles finished in second place with a 7–3 record but ran the table at home, going 6–0. The Eagles followed up with 12-game seasons in 1948 and

1949 and once again went 6–0 both years. The next time they won all their home games was in 1992, when they went 8–0.

The Eagles came close to winning all their home games in 1953 when they were 5–0–1. They tied Washington, 21–21, under the lights at Connie Mack Stadium. The Eagles trailed, 21–14, in the fourth quarter when Adrian Burk scored on a 1-yard quarterback sneak and Bobby Walston kicked the extra point. There was no two-point conversion and no overtime at that time.

The Eagles have nine years where they only lost one game at home: 1944, 1947, 1954, 1959, 1960, 1980, 2002, 2004, and 2017.

Four times the Eagles come close to winning all of their road games, losing just once. Playing six games away from home, the Eagles' lone loss in 1949 came when they were beaten by the Bears at Wrigley Field, 38–21. In 1960, the Eagles' only road loss was in a snowstorm in Pittsburgh, 27–21. The game meant nothing to the Eagles because they had clinched the Eastern Division title a week earlier. After playing seven away games from 1961 to 1977, the NFL expanded the schedule to 16 games in 1978. Only twice have they come close to running the table on the road. They had a lone loss on the road in 2001 at San Francisco, 13–3, and two years later, their only away loss came at Dallas, 23–21.

Sweeping your divisional games isn't as easy as it seems. Only twice have the Eagles won all their games against teams in their division. The first was in 1949 when they were 8–0 against the New York Bulldogs, New York Giants, Pittsburgh Steelers, and Washington Redskins. The Eagles had ten division games from 1950 to 1960 and it was increased to twelve in 1961. This arrangement only lasted six years when it was cut back to ten games from 1967 to '69.

When the NFL and AFL merged in 1970, the Eagles had only eight division games each year through 2001 when it was reduced to six games in 2002. The only year the Eagles went 6–0 in their division was 2004.

39 1934 and 1948.

The Eagles won only four of 11 games in 1934 but in all four wins they blanked their opponent. First, they shut out the Steelers in Pittsburgh, 17–0. In their second shutout, the Eagles set the NFL record for the most points scored in a shutout game with a 64–0 win over Cincinnati at Temple Stadium. The Eagles closed their season with two straight shutouts, 13–0, at Brooklyn and back at Baker Bowl, they blanked the Giants, 6–0.

The Eagles also posted four shutouts during the 1948 regular season when they won their first NFL title. They shut out the Giants at Shibe Park and Washington at Griffith Stadium in consecutive weeks, both by a score of 45–0. The Eagles third shutout that year came against the Boston Yanks and again it was by 45–0 at Shibe Park. The fourth shutout came at home, 17–0, over the Steelers. They also blanked the Chicago Cardinals, 7–0, in the NFL Championship Game at Shibe Park.

Only once have they shut out the same team twice in a season and it came when they blanked the New York Bulldogs twice in 1949. The Boston Yanks had moved to New York before the 1949 season. They played their games at the Polo Grounds. The Bulldogs first-ever game was against the Eagles and the Birds shut them out in the pouring rain, 7–0, at the Polo Grounds. Two months later back at Shibe Park, the Eagles shut out the Bulldogs again, 42–0.

A year later, the Bulldogs changed their name to Yankees and moved their home games to Yankee Stadium where they stayed for two years. New York was a Giants town and the club moved to Dallas in the 1952 season. That didn't work out very well as the club drew fewer than 15,000 per game. The owners turned the team back to the league and they were based in Hershey and played their remaining games on the road. They faced the Eagles at Shibe Park and the Birds came away with a 38–21 win. The following year, they became the Baltimore Colts, playing in their sixth season in four different cities at five different home sites.

40 The 1948 team set the club record for scoring 40 or more points in a game five times. The Eagles also scored 40 or more points in two straight games twice. The Eagles also set the club record for the most touchdowns scored in a season with 50. The record, which was set in a 12-game season, held up until 2013 when they played 16 games and scored 53 touchdowns. They topped that a year later by scoring 54 touchdowns.

After starting the season with a 21–14 loss to the Cardinals in Chicago and heading out to Los Angeles and squandering a 28–0 lead as the Rams came back and tied the game, 28–28, the Eagles took off. First they posted two of their four shutouts that season by blanking the New York Giants, 45–0, at Shibe Park and heading down to the nation's capital and keeping Washington off the scoreboard with another 45–0 shutout. The Eagles followed up by finally beating the Bears for the first time since joining the NFL in 1933, 12–7. The Eagles followed that by scoring at least 30 points in four straight, the final two, a 45–0 blanking of the Boston Yanks, then a 42–21 rout of Washington, both at Shibe Park. In the final game of the season, the Eagles went over 40 points for the fifth time as they beat the Lions, 45–21. This was the most points the Eagles scored in their last regular season game. The Eagles led, 24–21, in the fourth quarter when they broke it open with three touchdowns. Jack Ferrante, who caught three touchdown passes in the game, caught a 15-yard pass from Tommy Thompson who completed 16 of 28 passes for 258 yards and four touchdowns. Jim Parmer scored on a 42-yard run and Ferrante caught another touchdown pass from Thompson, this one for 23 yards.

The 2014 Eagles set the club record with nine games of scoring 30 or more points, breaking the record of eight which the 1948 team had in a 12-game season and it was tied in 2008. The Eagles started off the season with an Opening Day victory over Jacksonville at Lincoln Financial Field, 34–17, and a week later went to Indianapolis and beat the Colts, 30–27. Back home the following week, the Eagles knocked off Washington, 37–34. In the fifth game of the season, the Eagles beat the St. Louis Rams, 34–28, at the Linc. Four weeks later, the Eagles once again went over 30 points in back-to-back games. First they beat the Texans in Houston, 31–21, and beat Carolina back home, 45–21. After losing to the Packers at Lambeau Field, 53–20, the Eagles again went over 30 points in two straight games starting with a 43–24 win over Tennessee at home and followed that by going down to Dallas and defeating the Cowboys, 33–10. The ninth time was the final game of the season when they beat the New York Giants, 34–26, at MetLife Stadium.

ACKNOWLEDGMENTS

I would like to thank Merrill Reese, Ben Reese, and Alex Zerdel for their help in putting this book together.

Among the publications that were of great assistance were: team media guides for the Cleveland Browns, Dallas Cowboys, Green Bay Packers, New York Giants, Philadelphia Eagles, and Pittsburgh Steelers, *NFL Record & Fact Book*, *The Official NFL Encyclopedia*, *The Eagles Encyclopedia* by Ray Didinger and Robert S. Lyons, *Sunday's Warriors* by Donald P. Campbell, as well as "This Date in Philadelphia Eagles History," compiled by the author for WBCB Radio in Levittown, Pennsylvania.

ABOUT THE AUTHOR

Skip Clayton hosts *Racing Wrap*, a weekly one-hour radio show on WBCB Levittown, Pennsylvania, and has covered sports for the ABC Radio Network for more than forty years. Clayton is also the author of *Philadelphia's Big Five* and coauthor of *Tales from the Miami Dolphins Sideline* and *50 Phabulous Phillies*. He resides in Sellersville, Pennsylvania, with his wife, Joanne.